BEAT STRESS A...

WELBECK
BALANCE

ENDORSEMENTS

"Although the focus of Mark's excellent book is balancing ambition and anxiety in the workplace, these two themes could equally apply in other areas of life, especially sport. Firstly, self-improvement and progress must always begin with an honest assessment of your strengths and weaknesses. Secondly, life doesn't always deal in straight lines; it will always throw up a curve ball or two. It's how champions react and deal with these pressured situations that really counts."
Sir Clive Woodward, OBE – Former England rugby player, coach of 2003 World Cup winning England rugby team, author of *Winning!*

"This insightful book highlights the importance of moving from reactive to preventative measures in addressing mental health. It ably demonstrates the value of identifying individual purpose to build greater resilience. It's an invaluable handbook for those seeking to combat stress at any stage in their career."
Leena Nair – Chief Human Resources Officer, Unilever, and Member of the Leadership Executive

"Part autobiography and part lessons learned in the quest for success, this book will appeal to those who want workable ways to manage their personal stressors and strengthen their professional prowess without the need for wellness gurus and psychobabble!"
Dr Audrey Tang – Chartered Psychologist, award-winning author of *The Leader's Guide to Resilience*

"Mark does a first-class job of treating his breakdown as a breakthrough. Instead of brushing it under the carpet, he used his experience to learn about himself and then used this enhanced self-awareness as a platform to achieve his ambitions. The practical frameworks in this book provide us all with tools we can use to do the same."
Geoff McDonald – Mental Health Campaigner, Co-Founder of Minds@Work (focused on reducing stigma of mental health in the workplace)

"A lovely book: gentle and readable; accessible and relatable. I identified with a number of issues it raises and it made me think about decisions I've made and situations I've got myself into throughout my life and my career. More importantly, it offers practical things I can do to look after my mental health."
Michael Divers – People Director, Sir Robert McAlpine

"Rich with lessons from a deeply personal journey into the abyss of burnout and back, this book is an insightful and inspiring read for anyone facing stress in the workplace."
Dr Mithu Storoni – Eye surgeon and neuroscience researcher, author of *Stress Proof*

"A practical toolkit for ambitious people who don't want their mental health struggles to negatively impact their careers. Probably the most powerful learnings come from the author's strikingly honest account of how he battled his way back from severe mental illness and supported his daughter through a six-year fight against anorexia. This is a book that underlines the value of resilience."
Sally Percy – Business and finance journalist, contributor to *Forbes* and author of *Reach the Top in Finance*

"Like all aspects of mental fitness, we can empower ourselves to take control of our own unique stress response and identify when it is helping us to be at our best and when it is getting in the way – or worse, leading us towards burnout. The journey from insight to action is very well expressed through Mark's words. An important book and an essential read."
Kate Hesk – Chief People Officer, Cognomie (whose goal is to improve the world's Mental Fitness)

"This book is a remarkable resource that offers accessible anecdotes, insightful research and useful strategies to take control of our own mental health. It makes mental health care as normal as brushing teeth."
Zoë Routh – Author of Australian Business Book of the Year 2020, *People Stuff*

ABOUT THE AUTHOR

Mark Simmonds is a management trainer and consultant, operating in the areas of creativity and innovation. He has worked with a large number of international companies including Unilever, Johnson & Johnson, Pernod Ricard, HSBC, GlaxoSmithKline, Philips, Tesco and the Red Cross. He now runs a boutique agency, GENIUS YOU.

Throughout his life, Mark has struggled with anxiety, and back in 2001, he experienced a nervous breakdown, brought on by work-related stress. This culminated in four months' sick leave and a failed attempt on his own life. From rock bottom, he rebuilt a life – and career – that worked for him.

Mark now shares what he has learnt through his own journey with others, encouraging people to consider their mental wellbeing alongside their career aspirations. He is a regular contributor to the topic of mental health in the press, and has appeared on both local and national media.

Along with his son, Jack, he developed a YouTube channel (Mental Health Mark) designed to help professionals preserve their wellbeing.

Mark is married to Mel and they have two other children, Will and Emily. They also have two pets, a cat called Maisie and a dog called Peggy, both slightly bonkers!

BEAT STRESS AT WORK

HOW TO BALANCE YOUR AMBITION WITH YOUR ANXIETY

MARK SIMMONDS

Foreword by
Melissa Doman, M.A.

WELBECK
BALANCE

Published in 2022 by Welbeck Balance
An imprint of Welbeck Trigger Ltd
Part of Welbeck Publishing Group
Based in London and Sydney.
www.welbeckpublishing.com

Updated edition of *Breakdown and Repair*, first published by Trigger Publishing, an
Imprint of Shaw Callaghan Ltd in 2019.

Design and layout © Welbeck Trigger Ltd 2022
Text © Mark Simmonds 2022

A CIP catalogue record for this book is available from the British Library

ISBN
Trade Paperback – 978-1-80129-012-8

Illustrations by Lucy Streule

Typeset by Lapiz Digital Services
Printed in Great Britain by CPI Group (UK) Ltd, Croydon CRO 4YY

10 9 8 7 6 5 4 3 2 1

www.welbeckpublishing.com

To all the "Warriors" out there who have experienced mental ill health and who are willing to share their stories openly with the rest of the world.

FOREWORD

Mark's story needs to be told. It's powerful, authentic and gives a voice to so many others who've experienced something similar.

It reminds me of countless stories I've heard in my previous clinical counselling practice, and my current organizational psychology work with companies of all sizes around mental health in the workplace.

Stories of great achievement coupled with a complex rollercoaster of emotions that would give an MC Escher painting a run for its money.

Stories of bright, shining career stars that went *pop* because they missed the signs of their body and mind screaming at them to pause and notice the need for support.

Stories of people who were "quietly" struggling, who kept their experiences under lock and key from their colleagues for fear of the social judgment or misunderstanding they felt would inevitably come.

Stories of square pegs being shoved into round holes (e.g. the wrong job, company, or industry for them) that resulted in the self-critical "I must be the problem" mindset. Stories that stay with me still and that I keep in mind with every single event that I do around mental health at work.

A successful and passionate professional who cares deeply for his work and his family, Mark has struggled – and continues to struggle – intensely with his mental health, so much so that we almost didn't have him with us today, but I am deeply grateful that we do.

In this book, Mark uses what he has learnt to help others. I believe Mark genuinely wants readers to understand the following: *balancing a career, mental health and personality is no easy task – but it IS possible, and worth the work.*

Through his own experiences and a "pay it forward" mentality, Mark wants to do his part to reduce the number of times people get batted around in the real-life pinball machine called our "career path". His honest and raw story about the intersection of his mental health struggles, career, family and the intense challenges he encountered is inspiring because he gave himself the permission to be imperfect – to try to survive and figure out life, as we all do.

My hope for the readers of this book is that they find takeaways from Mark's story that are personal to them, and that they can use the guidance within to help shape their own paths. Millions upon millions of people have similar stories to Mark, and hopefully after reading this book, they will feel moved to share them, too – and be insightful and courageous enough to make career choices based on what is best for their mental health.

In my work with companies, I've repeatedly said that it will take a chorus of voices to make true change in the mental-health-at-work narrative, and everyone needs to do their part. Mark is a loud voice, doing his part. Sharing his vulnerability, where he wishes he had done things differently and encouraging us to prioritize our mental health, not the career ladder.

Melissa Doman, M.A.
Organizational Psychologist, Former Clinical Mental Health Therapist & Author of Yes, You Can Talk About Mental Health at Work

CONTENTS

Introduction   xv

1 It's in Your Genes
Look back in life to handle stress in the future   1

2 A Round Peg in a Round Hole
Find a close match between your personality and
your career   14

3 Drip, Drip, Drip, Drip
Minimize the destructive impact of "bad"
stress at work   41

4 The Unsettled Mind
Understand how a stress-related nervous
breakdown feels   64

5 Deep Depression and Big Decisions
Get support when making decisions during a
depressive episode   86

6 Resurfacing into the Workplace
Obtain the right professional guidance after a
period of mental illness   109

7 Happy Career Planning
Plan a career path that matches strengths
with opportunities   130

8 The Resilience Muscle
Embrace difficult challenges to build your
inner strength   155

9 The Explorer's Mindset
Enjoy business adventures while protecting
mental wellbeing   179

10 The Covid Curveball
Learn the lessons Covid-19 taught us about stress   199

Final Thoughts   219

Acknowledgements   224
References   225
Useful Resources   233

INTRODUCTION

I'm good at stress. I mean *really* good. Always have been. I get stressed watching my favourite soccer team, Brighton, play. I get stressed whenever I'm late for anything or when others are late. I get frustrated and then stressed playing golf with friends. I was stressed at the births of each of my three children, and then got stressed waiting anxiously for their exam results as they grew up.

I was that embarrassing touchline dad, always cursing the referee. And, quite amazingly, I often get stressed because there is nothing to be stressed about.

You see, the problem is that, historically, all the stress points listed above have conspired to inflame my anxiety, and this has caused me differing degrees of discomfort. I seem to have spent large chunks of my life feeling acutely uncomfortable. I was born with what I like to call my "Worry gene", which has always been close by my side, buzzing around like an irritating little fly that just refuses to leave you alone.

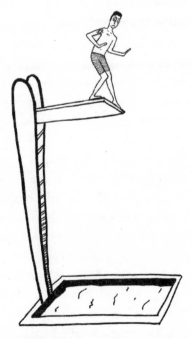

THE FEAR & THE GLORY

MENTAL HEALTH FACTS

- In 2020, a record 43% of workers across the world reported experiencing stress on a daily basis, increasing from 38% in 2019.
- US and Canadian workforces saw the highest levels of daily stress at a figure of 57%.
- In the UK alone, 828,000 people experienced work-related stress, depression or anxiety in 2019/2020 and 17.9 million working days were lost as a result.

Sources: Gallup: State of the Global Workplace Report; Labour Force Survey

But that's not the full story. I also have a competitive streak and am ambitious by nature. I want Brighton to be the best team in the division. I want to win at golf. I wanted my children to excel on the academic front, on the sports field and in their various dancing/singing competitions. And this has been the root of my problem. Although burdened by my Worry gene, I've also been "blessed" by my "Winner gene", and they don't make for great roommates. They're often in conflict, squabbling with each other, trying to get the upper hand; and the person caught in the crossfire is always me. It's these battles between the Winner and Worry genes, the collisions between my ambition and my anxiety, that have caused me the greatest amount of stress. (I'll come back to the Winner and Worry genes later, as they deserve a bit more explanation.)

Fortunately, I have survived. Just. There have been many close calls, particularly in the workplace, when the tension between the two genes has often been at its most intense. By failing to balance the needs of both, I've sometimes found myself stuck in situations where the stress needle edges into the red zone, and life starts to become difficult. But as I tiptoe toward my

60th year, I think I've found a few answers. I also believe that I have found some inner peace, with a truce of sorts now existing between these two conflicting aspects of my personality.

In fact, it's even better than that. In a career spanning almost 30 years, I can honestly say that I've never felt more energized than I do today. So much so that I sometimes wish I could rewind the career clock and start all over again.

WHY AM I WRITING THIS BOOK?

Let me begin by being clear about why I am *not* writing this book. It's not my intention to eliminate stress from your life – I can't promise that. But let me use a tennis analogy to explain what this book might achieve realistically. Beating stress at work is akin to Roger Federer wanting to win against Novak Djokovic more times than he loses. And vice versa. Both players are always attempting to develop strategies that will give them the upper hand whenever they play each other. But they don't expect for a moment that one victory will result in the other player abandoning the game forever. The main purpose of this book is to give you, the reader, some ideas for how you might be able to beat stress more often than it beats you. That feels achievable.

There are three other reasons why I am writing this book:

Firstly, even though great progress has been made in the area of mental health, far too many workers still experience the curse of work-related stress, and far too many working days are lost as a result. Organizations need to be much better at promoting a greater awareness and understanding of stress in the workplace. They are also duty bound to create a healthy climate that allows individuals to be honest about their mental health struggles. At the time of writing, Simone Biles, the American gymnast, has just pulled out of various competitions at the Tokyo Olympics in order to protect her wellbeing. She showed great courage in doing so. Wouldn't it be great if this openness was actively encouraged in all walks of life and received no more or less publicity than if somebody had suffered a serious physical injury? This crusade must be everybody's responsibility, and my book wants to play its small part.

The second reason for writing this book is that I have spent the majority of my career in management training, working with young managers from major corporations like Unilever, Philips, GlaxoSmithKline, Tesco and HSBC. I love encouraging others to develop their skills in the areas of creativity and innovation. And I would be delighted if I could help the same kind of people become more aware of their relationship with stress, and enhance their skill set so they can cope with it more effectively.

Thirdly, I want to help people in need, plain and simple. Calling it a legacy would sound too pompous, but if a lifetime's experience at the coalface could benefit just a handful of people, it would constitute success in my mind. And one of my specific aims is to provide some concrete guidance on how to turn off the "bad stress" tap, a term I will explain in more detail later in the book.

"What mental health needs is more sunlight, more candour, more unashamed conversation."

Glenn Close, actor

WHO THIS BOOK IS FOR

I hope this book will help professionals of all ages and levels of experience: those who have left education and are dipping their toes into the world of work, and those with two or three years' work experience under their belt and are finding the corporate scene more mentally challenging than they had bargained for (in my view, the sooner this cohort learns how to deal with stress, the better). The book will be of equal help to more experienced professionals who want to better manage stress in their current roles, or those who want to climb the corporate ladder; and to the more adventurous types who want a taste of the unpredictable world of self-employment.

HOW THIS BOOK WORKS

This book is a hybrid. On the one hand, it's the story of my struggles with stress and clinical anxiety throughout my working life, with plenty of twists and turns, and ups and downs. On the other hand, it's a practical self-help book, providing a myriad of tips, checklists and frameworks. But I do need to make it clear that this is *my* story, and I will share the things that worked for *me*. I don't want to give the false impression that the book is any kind of blueprint, a prescriptive set of guidelines that you must follow if you want to rid yourself of stress forever. It isn't, and it won't. I just invite you to digest the content and extract the bits that resonate most with you, based on your own experiences.

I am fortunate to have been given the opportunity to work very closely with Melissa Doman, M.A., an Organizational Psychologist and former Clinical Mental Health Therapist, and author of *Yes, You Can Talk About Mental Health at Work: Here's Why (and How To Do It Really Well)*. She has used her significant clinical and organizational experience to make sure that I have been duly diligent with what I have said and how I have said it, both in terms of accuracy and intentionality. The difference between saying the right and wrong thing around the topics of stress and mental health can often be subtle, and she has kept me on the right side of the line.

The book is also injected with plenty of inspiring quotations, relevant analogies and research-based statistics, as well as case studies from people who have been willing to share their stories of mental health and stress in the workplace. If, by being open and honest about our experiences of mental ill health, we can encourage others to do the same, then maybe the mental health crusade will start to gather even more momentum. That will be a really good thing.

And, finally, the illustrations dotted all over the book, drawn by the wonderfully talented Lucy Streule, will hopefully bring a smile to your face. Although talking about chronic stress, anxiety and depression can have its dark moments, I wanted to bring a lightness of touch to the narrative to make it more digestible.

This is a book to be enjoyed rather than endured because, at its core, it's underpinned by a big bucketful of optimism.

1

IT'S IN YOUR GENES

Look back in life to handle stress in the future

In the world of business, future strategies and tactics need to be rooted in historic performance – and the same principle applies at a personal level. This chapter will explore how your experiences of stress and anxiety in the past could provide some clues as to the kind of relationship you might have with them going forward.

I will examine three themes:

1. **The role of your genetic footprint:** How much can you attribute to your genes as far as the make-up of your personality and the workings of your brain are concerned? Can you be naturally disposed to experiencing stress more easily or developing clinical anxiety?
2. **The impact of environment:** What role do your immediate surroundings play in the development of your personality? Are you permanently affected by any stressful behaviours displayed by your parents during your childhood or your interactions with them over the years?
3. **The "tricky gene" trail:** How do "tricky" genes get passed down from one generation to the next?

The nature versus nurture debate has been raging for hundreds of years and it still remains inconclusive. Although it has long been accepted that certain physical characteristics like the colour of your eyes, pigmentation of your skin or the straightness of your hair are all a function of the genes you inherit, it has now been agreed that certain behavioural tendencies, personality attributes, and mental and physical abilities are also hardwired in before we see the light of day. Research has shown that conditions like schizophrenia, bipolar disorder, anxiety and depression can all be passed down from generation to generation.

As far as nurture is concerned, the list of non-genetic contributors to mental ill health include factors like trauma in early life, living in a dysfunctional home, parental favouritism, and physical or sexual abuse. Your upbringing undoubtedly plays a significant role in the way you learn how to think and feel.

So herein lies the question. If you experience excessive amounts of stress or anxiety, do you attribute this to how your brain was configured by the time you popped out of your mother's womb or to the way in which you have been affected by the environmental factors in your life so far? In other words, when you wake up every morning feeling really stressed about work and dreading the day ahead, do you hold either nature or nurture accountable? Or both?

"Nature or nurture? Either way, it's your parents' fault."

Matthew P. Normand, Professor of Psychology

NATURE AND NURTURE IN ACTION TOGETHER

Alicja (Alice) Pomiechowska, my mother, was born in Kolno, Poland, in 1933. During the Second World War, when she was eight years old, she was forced to flee across the border along with her mother, Jadwiga, and younger brother, Valdemar. Her father was missing in action. The three of them ended up enduring freezing cold winters stuck in Siberian refugee camps.

They spent the rest of the war in misery, living in dire conditions, existing rather than anything else. But they survived, and when the war was over, my grandmother decided they would resettle in Kenya, one of the countries that had agreed to accept refugees. My mother's teenage years were spent in poverty in the port of Mombasa, where she took on the responsibility of looking after her brother while my grandmother worked as a nurse to earn the money they needed to live on. My mother learned to speak English and eventually found work as a secretary in Nairobi; there she met and married my father, Peter, who was working for Pearl Assurance as a British expatriate.

As far as my mother was concerned, it was a romantic ending of sorts to what had been a challenging start to life.

MENTAL HEALTH FACTS

- Depression is a mental disorder that affects over 300 million people worldwide and, according to the World Health Organization, it costs the global economy as much as $1 trillion annually.
- In the world's largest investigation into the impact of DNA on mental health, more than 200 researchers identified at least 44 gene variants that raised the risk of depression.
- A 2018 study found that children with anxiety disorders were three times more likely to have at least one parent who had an anxiety disorder.

Sources: Major Depressive Disorder Working Group of the Psychiatric Genomics Consortium; European and Child Adolescent Study

In her early 1950s, when the family was back in the UK, my mother had a severe nervous breakdown from which she never really recovered. She was diagnosed with clinical depression and chronic anxiety. The last 30 years of her life were spent in "hermit-like" solitude, isolating herself from society for her own self-protection. She survived on a diet of antidepressants, anti-anxiety pills and sleeping tablets, in an attempt to keep both the depression at bay and her nerves under control. Was her anxiety born out of nature or was it a direct result of the trauma and chilling experiences she endured during her childhood when nothing remained certain for long? Or was it both?

She adopted three mechanisms for coping with her anxiety and her daily stresses. Firstly, she did her best to avoid any situations that brought uncertainty; secondly, she smoked like a chimney; and thirdly, later in her life, she resorted to a cocktail of anti-anxiety medications. Life seemed to be one perpetual challenge for my mother, a never-ending struggle, and when she eventually passed away, aged 81, I got the distinct feeling it was somewhat of a relief for her.

My father, Peter, was a very cautious man, and this manifested itself not only in the workplace, where he remained a loyal one-company man for the entirety of his career, but also at home. His weekends were metronomic in nature. Back home from London at 6.30pm on a Friday. First whisky at 7pm. Last whisky at 9pm, followed by lightly poached eggs on toast. In bed by 11.15pm. A walk on Brighton seafront first and last thing on Saturday, repeated on Sunday. Light stretching at the end of both days. Paperwork always filed away, every penny accounted for. Bedroom immaculate, with slippers neatly in place, socks and underpants carefully ironed. My father was never late for anything. Ever.

Pause for Thought

1. Did either of your parents have a diagnosed mental illness that you know of? Or do you suspect they had one that was never diagnosed?
2. How did your parents respond in stressful situations? Can you remember any particular behaviours they exhibited?
3. Would you say that either of your parents were chronic worriers by nature?

In fact, he was more than that. He was a "you can never arrive too early" kind of person. Before entering the world of work, my father served as a Royal Marine, where strict orders and tight discipline would have been his daily diet.

MY "WORRY GENE"

So, right up until the time I went to university, I lived in a household that breathed my mother's crippling anxiety and my father's extreme caution. My amateur psychologist hunch is that the latter was down to nature whereas the former was probably more down to a mix of nature and nurture. Whichever it was, this combination gave birth to my "Worry gene".

There were plenty of early warning signs during my teenage years that the "Worry gene" was flowing through my bloodstream. At school, I was a conscientious student, preparing myself thoroughly for exams, never leaving things until the last minute, and always heavily dependent on meticulous revision timetables. My peers would be burning the midnight oil, drinking strong coffee and cramming, while I was tucked up in bed at 10pm, fully prepared for the challenges of the day ahead. This was a sign not of complacency, but of extreme caution. It was "helpful Worry" in action.

But I was also often excessively anxious about failing, letting down myself and others around me. Socially, I was painfully nervous and verbally clumsy in and around members of the opposite sex. My incessant nail-biting, greasy hair and chronic acne, all part of a teenager's hormonal mix, didn't help matters either. This was "unhelpful Worry" in action.

MY "WINNER GENE"

What complicated matters was that I possessed a core personality trait that worked in the opposite direction to the "Worry gene" – my "Winner gene". I was a very competitive person, both in the classroom and on the sports field. I was

LOUISA'S STORY

The burden and blessing of the past

As a child, my father told me consistently that I lacked confidence. When I left university, my General Anxiety Disorder and Rejection Sensitive Dysmorphia (most likely inherited from my mother and exacerbated by the trauma of her premature death when I was 14) were still undiagnosed. Burdened by an average degree, an ineptitude for maths, a fear of interviews and poor self-esteem, I applied for roles in the corporate world for which I was completely ill-suited.

In hindsight, I should have listened to the advice of my school careers advisor, who told me to become a librarian or to seek a vocational path. But, instead, I focused on roles expected of me as the first graduate in my family. I suspect I was also in search of recognition from a successful, entrepreneurial father who struggled to show love.

I was destined to fail. It took decades in roles that challenged my anxiety, as well as an unplanned "education" received by raising our neurodivergent son, for me to recognize the dangers of setting unrealistic expectations. The truth of the matter is that the work we are passionate about is key to our happiness/ success. Looking back, the roles I have been most comfortable in and fulfilled by have been the ones that stimulated the creative part of my brain, or in which I've been able to work autonomously.

Research has demonstrated that the trauma of losing a parent as a child may impede the development of children, impacting their mental health, relationships and earning potential. On the plus side, it teaches resilience and compassion – strengths that may not be recognized in the engine room of corporations, but are nonetheless incredibly powerful in the industry of caring for others.

blessed with above-average talent in several different team sports, including rugby and cricket, and competing and winning were always important to me. I am not sure whether my aptitude for sport or my desire to win were a result of nature or nurture. Neither my mother or father had a sporting background, so maybe this was a classic case of genes skipping a generation?

Unfortunately, there were too many fundamental differences between the "Worry" and the "Winner genes", too many conflicts of interest in terms of what they valued. My inability to relax when under pressure meant I never quite fulfilled my potential, particularly on the sports field, where my mental fragility often let me down at crucial moments. When my mind needed to be relaxed in the heat of battle, it was often swamped with negative thoughts and irrational doubts, neither of which were conducive to the art of winning.

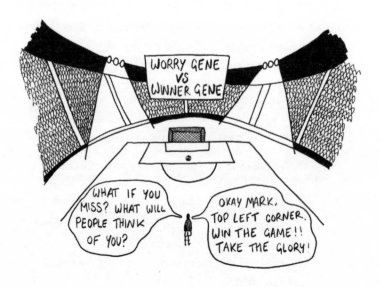

I would not have been the person to take the last-minute penalty to win the soccer World Cup final or serve out for the match in a tense fifth set in the Wimbledon final. There would have been far too much distracting chatter going on in my head at the time.

All of this should have provided me with some early evidence that I would need to manage my hopes and expectations carefully if the marriage between the two genes was going to remain a stable one. When I grew up and entered the hurly-burly world of business, I would find out just how important it was to carefully balance the contrasting needs of both. One day in the distant future, not doing so would almost cost me my life.

Before going any further, I need to establish a point of fact. You won't find the "Winner" or "Worry genes" listed in a medical dictionary. It's just that, to a layman like me, they seem to embody the emotional states that accurately sum up two opposing forces that exist in my mind. Although they cannot be classified as genes in any scientific sense, they feel intrinsic to my DNA. They both remain close to my heart because the three of us have been through a lot together.

I will stick with them during the rest of the book, and from now on, will refer to them as Winner and Worry.

Pause for Thought

1. Think back to when you were a teenager. Which specific stressful situations do you remember most? Why were they so stressful?
2. Can you remember how you reacted under pressure? Which behaviours did you show?
3. What did you think at the time? How did the stress make you feel?

THE "TRICKY GENE" TRAIL

Here's an interesting observation: "tricky" genes are not always shared out evenly within families. My grandmother and uncle had endured the same atrocities and hardships as my mother in the refugee camps of Siberia and Kenya, but they both remained mentally robust and resilient. In fact, my grandmother's adventures continued when she decided to emigrate to the USA in her mid-life, where she met and married a Texan oilman called George and lived happily and healthily until the ripe old age of 90. She was as tough as nails, not averse to taking risks and always curious to know what lay round the next corner in life.

> *"Your genetics load the gun. Your lifestyle pulls the trigger."*
>
> Mehmet Oz, television personality and surgeon

My mother wasn't. Did she inherit her "tricky" genes from somebody higher up in the family tree? And were these triggered by the challenging environments she found herself in at different stages of her life?

Within my own family, Emily, my daughter, found herself on the "tricky gene" trail when she became seriously ill with anorexia nervosa, aged 16. At its core, this is an intense anxiety disorder. Although it was difficult to pin down the precise origins of her condition, it is generally recognized that high-achieving perfectionists are often susceptible to eating disorders. All it took with Emily was the arrival of a perfect storm of external events, coalescing together to activate her perfectionist streak. Exam pressure, the death of a favourite teacher, glandular fever, an eye-opening trip to a poverty-stricken part of Ghana in Africa, as well as some self-critical body image problems, were the catalysts. And no doubt her exposure to the proliferation of social media platforms might well have contributed to the onset of her eating disorder; the link between the two is now backed up by plenty of research studies.

As a result, Emily was unable to take her A-Level exams, spent a year in three eating disorder clinics, self-harmed, threatened suicide, and experienced severe clinical depression and anxiety. Her weight dropped to 32kg (70lb), and at her lowest point she had a tube inserted into her nose to give her the nutrition she needed to stay alive.

My theory is that my mother, myself and my daughter represented the fault line down the family "tricky gene" trail. Our mental ill health was not a choice. Neither my mother, my daughter nor I chose to have our various mood or eating disorders. And, I don't want to give the impression that these "tricky genes" have been a burden, bringing nothing but misery and suffering. This is not the case. Yes, they have been unhelpful at times, for sure, and often difficult to manage, but as I have got older, I have begun to view them as much a blessing as a burden, because they bring to the party life-enriching qualities such as empathy, resilience, insight and understanding.

And the world could certainly do with more of those, couldn't it?

HELP YOURSELF

TRY THE PRESSURE AUDIT

As I mentioned earlier, businesses should always take a long hard look at the past to help them make the right decisions. When you start tip-toeing out into the world of work, you can also tap into your teenage years and early 20s to better understand how you tackled stress during that period. This may help you in the future. The Pressure Audit provides a simple framework for getting some helpful feedback. Here is how it applied to myself:

Pressure Audit

"At exam time, you were always extremely conscientious and well-prepared."
MOTHER

"You hated the thought that you might let other people down."
FAMILY FRIEND

What was your impression of me when I found myself in pressure situations?

"I remember that you always used to get very anxious before big matches."
BROTHER

"You didn't always cope very well when things started to go wrong."
SCHOOL FRIEND

WHAT TO DO

1. Identify three or four people who have known you well during your life so far and who you trust to provide you with their honest perspective.
2. Ask them what their impression of you was when you found yourself in pressure situations.
3. Look for any patterns or commonalities in their responses and use this information to help you better predict how you *might* react to stressful situations in the business world in the future. This data might lead you to develop coping mechanisms for stress, and could make it easier to identify job environments where you are more likely to flourish and less likely to flounder.

A COUPLE OF WATCHOUTS

A. This information is qualitative rather than quantitative. It is only indicative.

B. You are not a slave to your past, and your response to stressful situations during your childhood does not necessarily reflect how you might respond to them in adulthood. Always give yourself the opportunity to grow and develop, and this includes the way you tackle stressful situations.

KEY TAKEAWAYS

- **Your hereditary inheritance:** This must take some responsibility, as it's not just about the colour of your eyes or the shade of your skin. Your tendency to worry, experience mood swings, and how you deal with stress are also swimming in the genetic pool.

- **A "tricky gene" trail exists in many families:** Not every family member has a predisposition to mental ill health. The trail can take a fairly random route down through the family tree.

- **Your home environment:** This plays a very influential role in the development of your core character and how you respond to stressful situations, particularly in your early years when you're still being moulded into shape by life itself.

2

A ROUND PEG IN A ROUND HOLE

Find a close match between your personality and your career

The greater the gap between the needs of your core personality and the demands of your job, and the more you are doing something that is "just not you", the more stressed you are likely to be. This is particularly the case if the gap stays too wide for too long. The chapter will focus on three themes:

1. **Treat your job like a relationship:** Remember that it's easier to make any kind of partnership with another person work the more you have in common with them. It's no different as far as your career is concerned.
2. **Seek alignment:** You'll have your own set of needs and motivations when it comes to your job. Your employer will also have their own. As early as possible in your career, develop a "nose" to help you decide if alignment exists between the two.

3. **Liking your job is a positive first step:** The more you enjoy your work, the more purposeful you find it, the more likely you will be able to avoid stress.

THE RIGHT FIT

At the time of writing, Eliud Kipchoge from Kenya holds the marathon world record time. He won the Berlin race in 2018, clocking a time of 2 hours, 1 minute and 39 seconds. He shattered the previous world record by 1 minute and 18 seconds. In a typical week, he wakes up at around 5am and runs between 200–225km (124–140 miles) per week, which is the equivalent of completing a marathon daily, Monday through to Friday.

In order to survive this kind of gruelling regime, it's obvious your shoes must fit your feet like a glove. If you are putting your lower limbs under that much pressure by wearing inappropriate footwear, sooner or later problems will emerge – runner's knee, Achilles tendinitis, plantar fasciitis and patellar tendonitis (great names!), iliotibial band syndrome (even better!) and the slightly more prosaic-sounding blisters, shin splints and ankle sprains.

"If you have to fold to fit in, it ain't right."

Yrsa Daily-Ward, writer

A whole industry caters for the specific demands of athletes who are serious about looking after their feet, and it is a question of performance enhancement as well as injury prevention. When Kipchoge subsequently became the first person to run the first sub-2-hour marathon, he was wearing the revolutionary Vaporfly running shoes, said to increase an athlete's energetic efficiency by 4% or more, a significant number in marathon terms.

So, what's the point of all this information about footwear? Well, this chapter will emphasize the importance of finding the right job (shoes) so that you can operate in an environment where you are better able to protect your mental health (feet) and limit undue suffering (painful blisters).

But, just to be clear, although well-fitting shoes are important to an athlete, they can still experience stress fractures by over-training or training in the wrong way. The same principle applies in the workplace. In other words, you might be in the right job, but you can still get stressed due to a number of other factors, like a heavy workload or a tricky boss.

THE PROLONGED PANIC ATTACK

In my early 20s, Worry and Winner got their first proper examination when I started working for Unilever, the global consumer goods company, co-headquartered in Rotterdam and London. It's one of the largest companies in the world, and its household brands, like Dove, Axe, Knorr, Magnum and Domestos, are available in around 190 countries.

Unilever also has one of the most respected management trainee programmes for young people who want to forge a career in marketing. I succeeded in joining it when I was 25, working for Birds Eye Wall's, one of its operating companies at the time, and I was pretty proud of my achievement. So was Winner – his high expectations were being met. The career roadmap was now neatly laid out in front of me and the future seemed bright. Trainee to Brand Manager to Marketing Manager to Marketing Director. Easy as 1,2,3.

The first few days, weeks and months were all fairly uneventful. I was a marketing trainee going through a series of job rotations, interspersed with residential training courses every few months or so. I was part of a cohort of new joiners, all as keen as mustard, dabbling in the world of big business for the first time, and desperately trying to look more important than we really were. Nobody was under great pressure to perform, there were no big expectations. We were on a steep learning curve and mistakes were quickly forgiven.

During this period, there wasn't sufficient evidence to help me decide whether I had landed the right job or not, and it was probably too early to be asking myself that kind of question anyway. After all, I was receiving the best early career development I could possibly ask for. That was surely enough. So, head down and just get on with it. The early feedback I received from my line managers was all very positive. I was ticking all the right boxes and heading in the "right direction".

Twelve months later, I found myself pacing up and down the basement of the Birds Eye Wall's building like a caged animal. I was alone, surrounded only by freezers full of frozen peas, beef burgers and fish fingers, and my own confused thoughts. I was trying to work out why I was suddenly feeling so anxious, why I seemed incapable of completing the most basic of tasks at my desk upstairs. I needed a bit of head space, away from people, to think clearly and work out what on earth was going on in my frazzled mind. I wasn't swamped by major decisions or weighed down under huge amounts of work pressure. At the time, I was only a trainee, the lowest of the low. Admittedly, I had been handed a little more responsibility and people were relying on me to get things done, but I was still a relatively insignificant cog in the wheel. I didn't know it at the time, but I was experiencing my first little blip.

A couple of weeks earlier, I had started fretting over every small decision, and with the increased fretting came further indecision. The more indecisive I became, the less productive I was. And the less productive I was, the longer it took me to work my way through the to-do list for the day.

I vividly remember one of my responsibilities was to ensure that all the copy on the packaging was completely accurate before thousands of packs were printed and distributed to the likes of Tesco and Sainsbury's. It was a thankless job, requiring great attention to detail. I always dreaded the call from some wise guy on the production line asking, with just a hint of mischief, whether the company was really selling "beef buggers" instead of "beef burgers". So, I would check, re-check and check again, a telltale sign of increasing anxiety.

FINDING SOLACE AMONGST
THE FROZEN PEAS

And then, one day, I looked at my to-do list and found myself incapable of doing anything on it. I froze. That's when the basement wandering started.

I had no idea what was happening to me. This had all come on very quickly, with no obvious warning signs. It had snuck in stealthily underneath the radar, and I became very fearful of the events that were slowly unfolding. It was an uncomfortable and lonely sensation that I had never experienced before.

At this time, I was sharing a two-bedroom flat in Wimbledon with my younger brother, Michael, a trainee accountant with Price Waterhouse. As I sat on the stairs at midnight, staring into space, unable to sleep, he just looked at me, worried and helpless. Caring for a brother who seemed to have lost the plot wasn't really his area of expertise.

Mel and I had now been going out together for just over three years. We had met in our first job after leaving university. Throughout this entire episode, I remember her, like my brother, being perplexed more than anything else. It felt a bit out of the blue for all of us. I decided to keep things quiet as far as my parents were concerned. The thought of my mother fretting and getting flustered would only have added to the pressure I was now under. It wouldn't have been fair on her either.

Pause for Thought

1. Pick one emotion that describes how you feel about your job right now.
2. How would you describe your current stress levels – mild, moderate or severe?
3. If your stress levels are rising, why do you think that is? What are you doing about it?

After a few days of further dithering, my to-do list was growing longer and longer, and I knew it would only be a matter of time before my co-workers began suspecting something was wrong. I considered approaching HR, but was worried, quite irrationally, that any admission of mental ill health would be the death knell of my Unilever career. In any case, what would I say to them? How would I explain what I was thinking and feeling when I wasn't even sure myself?

Finally, I bit the bullet and decided to confide in my boss. It would have been the last thing he wanted to hear. He was a well-organized and productive professional, but still had more than enough on his plate as it was. Mercifully, and without any hesitation, he told me to take a week off, get some help, and come back when I was feeling better. I'm sure he had a pretty good hunch what was happening, but he promised not to mention this to anyone else. Our little secret. That bought me some welcome breathing space. Later on in life, as mental health and wellbeing rose toward the top of the corporate agenda, I realized that the role of the line manager was a critical cog in the wheel. (More about this later in the book.) But at this point in time, I was just keen to brush this episode under the carpet and avoid getting rumbled.

MENTAL HEALTH FACTS

- Only 14% of 2,000 workers polled in 2019 said they felt comfortable discussing their mental health worries at work.
- Only 42% of those interviewed felt they would be able to talk openly about their physical conditions.
- While 70% of workers know basic physical first aid, only 36% feel that they are skilled enough to have a conversation about mental ill health.

Source: Mental Health First Aid England/Bauer Media Group

During my week off work, I went to see a doctor who told me that I'd had a prolonged panic attack. According to him, it was nothing more serious than that, quite common in fact. That made me feel better, less weird, and I didn't question his diagnosis. He prescribed me some medication for a few weeks and sent me on my way. I went back to work a week later, things improved slightly, but my enjoyment levels remained depressingly low. And that was that, for now. The storm had passed.

MEDICAL TERMS

I want to clarify a few medical terms that will keep popping up in the book as it is important to get these right.

Years later, when I experienced my "Big Blip", I found out from the psychiatrist treating me at the time that the correct medical term for my little blip was agitated depression. Although many people experience symptoms such as feeling slowed down and lethargic when they are depressed, others may experience the opposite. They may feel anything from restlessness and agitation to irritability and anger. Even fear. It's also known as "mixed mania" or "mixed features".

One of the causes of agitated depression is high levels of anxiety. Experiencing anxiety is a normal part of everyday life, but people with anxiety disorders frequently have persistent and excessive amounts of fear around everyday situations. There are a number of different anxiety disorders, including agoraphobia (the fear of being in places that might cause you to panic) and social anxiety disorder (the fear of being perceived badly or judged negatively by others). However, generalized anxiety disorder is the most common of all, characterized by persistent and excessive worry about everyday events.

And finally, stress, which in clinical terms isn't a mental illness diagnosis, but is defined as any type of change that causes physical, emotional or psychological strain.

So, if I can "play doctor" for a moment, my self-diagnosis would have gone something like this: "Mark is experiencing high levels of stress in the workplace and these have had an impact on his anxiety. This situation has remained unchecked for several weeks and, as a result, Mark has now developed agitated depression."

"GOOD" AND "BAD" STRESS

During those basement-wandering days, I felt frightened and agitated all the time. I was experiencing "bad stress". Back in 1908, two psychologists, Yerkes and Dodson discovered that mild electric shocks could be used to motivate rats to complete a maze, but when the shocks became too strong, they would start panicking and scurry around haphazardly in an attempt to escape. This became the basis of the Yerkes-Dodson Law, which suggested there is a clear link between performance and arousal. For example, an optimal amount of stress will help you focus on an exam and remember all the key facts. You might feel energized, stimulated, even exhilarated. This "good stress" might help you perform even better. But too much anxiety can impair your ability to remember anything worth writing down on the exam paper. You might freeze and become incapable of thinking straight. This "bad stress" might make you not perform at all. And this can happen to anyone. The Yerkes-Dodson Law applies in most areas of human performance. For what it's worth, I felt like that electrocuted rat.

"On this dark Sunday night, lying on the grass, staring at the sky ... I wonder if the stars get Monday blues too."

Saptarshi Nandy, author

A SQUARE PEG IN A ROUND HOLE ...

I proceeded to stumble my way through the next four years at Unilever, never completely comfortable in what I was doing, never performing at my best, always slightly anxious, on edge. It was gradually dawning on me that I wasn't destined for the higher echelons of the company, and I certainly wasn't viewed as fast-track material. Winner found that hard to swallow.

Although I did reach the first step on the corporate ladder when I was promoted to a brand manager, I couldn't ever claim to be a natural in that role. Mental health wise, nothing dramatic would happen during this period, and there were no more panic attacks or basement-wandering episodes. But there were plenty of Sunday evening blues and car journeys to work I wished would never end.

During this time, I tried doing Transcendental Meditation to halt my rising stress levels. I had become a sucker for self-help books in my quest for continual personal development, and many of them were now promoting the benefits of meditation. The approach had also been strongly recommended by my mother, who was using it to keep her anxiety at bay.

MIKE'S STORY

Finding the right career 25 years too late

I was Chief Financial Officer of a telecommunications company based in Sydney, a medium- sized business with 500 employees and offices across Australia. I was also head of IT, Legal and HR, with responsibility for almost 100 staff and 10 direct reports. I was financially successful and held in high regard by peers and friends alike. However, from the inside, I was dying – literally. I had endured various crises along the way, caused by the pressure of the role. Once I arrived home from work on a Friday with a big red blotch in the middle of my forehead, the result of stabbing myself with a pen in frustration. I spent a weekend medicated with sleeping pills, with my wife bringing me breakfast, lunch and dinner in bed, and by Monday I was ready for battle again.

My problem was that there was a mismatch between my personality and the demands of the job. I am deeply introverted, hate being the centre of attention, loathe any form of public speaking and, being totally frank, I am not blessed with huge amounts of empathy for my fellow human beings. The mismatch caused me enormous amounts of stress, and I had to resort to medication to help me cope.

On 30 June 2015, aged 48, I left the corporate world. In hindsight, if I could talk to my 22-year-old self, I would say, "Firstly, follow your passion. Secondly, really understand where your personal traits, both good and bad, are well suited." Five years later, I work for myself, trading stocks and shares. I have never been happier!

So, twice a day, morning and evening, I would sit down somewhere comfortable, close my eyes and repeat my unique mantra silently for 20 minutes. Over time, this practice was meant to bring tranquillity to my turbulent mind. But whenever I practised the technique shortly after waking up, my head was so crammed full of the jobs to be done in the day ahead that there was no space for the mantra to be heard. It was bullied out of the way by more dominating work thoughts. And when I got back home and attempted it again in the early evening, I was so mentally exhausted from the stresses and strains of the previous ten hours that I would quickly fall asleep after five or six repetitions of the mantra.

In my mid-20s, practices like meditation were still viewed as niche by the general population, something to turn to when all else failed. It certainly didn't enjoy the well-deserved reputation it has today as a progressive and holistic therapy.

Unfortunately, I wasn't doing Transcendental Meditation any justice – the stress of work was putting it under too much pressure to weave its magic on me. But, to be honest, the fact I had resorted to meditating in the first place suggested I wasn't addressing the root problem.

I had found myself in the wrong job. It wasn't either the company or the job that were to blame. Brand management in Unilever was and still is a great job. It just wasn't a great one for me. It was like one of those failing relationships that ends with one person saying: "I promise this has nothing to do with you. You're terrific. It's me. I'm the problem. Honest." Put another way, the shoes weren't fitting. In fact, nothing was fitting.

THE UNCOMFORTABLE FEELING OF A BAD FIT

Pause for Thought

1. If you are unhappy or stressed at work, why do you think that is?
2. Has this feeling emerged recently or is it part of a longer-term pattern?
3. Are you willing to try to identify the root cause of your current feelings and take action to change your situation?

DISCOVERING THE "SECRET OF LIFE"!?

Stick with me here and take this with a big pinch of salt, but I think I might have worked out the secret to a happy life! Here goes. There are 24 hours in a day. Let's assume you sleep for eight hours, work for eight hours, and relax for eight hours. Therefore, if you choose to be with a long-term partner, you can assume that the combined time spent at work and with your partner probably accounts for not far off 100% of the total time available.

So, this is the secret as far as I am concerned. As long as you are blessed with a good dose of health and a fair bit of luck, then your route to fulfilment is finding the right life partner, choosing the right career and sticking with both. The sooner, the better. And if it takes two or three goes at each quest, so be it. In my view, if you get these foundations right, you'll have a much better shot at keeping "bad" stress at bay.

After a courtship lasting almost six years, Mel agreed to marry me on a sunny May afternoon in Ascot, Berkshire. I was 29 and Mel had just turned 28. During our period of dating, Mel had borne witness to my little blip at Unilever, but I think she accepted this as part and parcel of being in your 20s. Everybody our age was still trying to find their feet, establish who they were and decide what they wanted out of life. Little did Mel know that she was also marrying Winner and Worry, and that she would be in for a bumpy ride.

Now, 25 years later, I can safely say this was the smartest move of my life. Mel is even-keeled. She doesn't do dramatic ups and downs, and in many ways she is my polar opposite, the calm millpond to my choppy waters. In the years ahead, the mental disorders of my mother, our daughter and me would sorely test her cheerful character. I had found half of my secret to a happy life, but I was still looking for the other half.

A PROFESSIONAL EPIPHANY MOMENT

After being at Unilever for just over three years, I was attending one of their excellent residential training programmes when I had a eureka moment that would change my professional life forever. I was taking part in a group exercise and my team chose me to present back our recommendations to the guest lecturer. I enjoyed the entire experience. Slightly stressful, yes, but stressful in an exhilarating, energizing kind of way. Good stress, not bad stress.

At the end of the session, the lecturer awarded a black-and-white branded T-shirt to the person he felt had made the most impactful presentation. That person turned out to be me. It wasn't a particularly big achievement in the grand scheme of things, but I was quietly chuffed, as was Winner.

"Don't wait for a light to appear at the end of the tunnel.
Stride down there and light the bloody thing yourself."

Sara Henderson, author

It was at this point that I realized I was fishing in the wrong pond. I should have been working in an educational role, where communicating with others was the key prerequisite. The part-time jobs I had enjoyed most when I was a student were working in schools that taught English as a foreign language. I loved those jobs with a passion, and was good at them. Teaching came naturally to me. So, the question I was now asking myself was why had I chosen a career path so removed from the kind of work that ticked all the boxes? Was it the pressure I placed on myself to get a well-paid corporate job rather than exist on a teacher's salary, trying to meet the imagined expectations of my parents and "pay them back" for their investment in me? After all, I had emerged from a top university with a 2:1 degree and my CV was saying all the right kinds of things. Everything was directing me down the conventional route, a career either in the City or in Big Industry.

But right now, I was just plain tired of sticking to what was "conventional". For the next 12 months, I embarked on a quest to find the job that was right for me. I desperately needed to find shoes that fitted, ones that didn't give me blisters and shin splints. At least now, I was moving in the right direction, searching for something in the educational space where I could leverage the commercial experience

THE CORPORATE CAGE

I had gained working at Unilever. On paper, that combination seemed to fit perfectly with my personality. Even though, during the months that followed, I would have to face countless rejections and plenty of disappointment, the fact I knew roughly where I was heading meant my stress levels subsided. I now sensed that the right job was out there somewhere waiting for me, and this gave me the strength I needed to soldier on in a job that wasn't for me.

A ROUND PEG IN A ROUND HOLE

It was a cold, wet morning in the first week of January. I was now 30 years old. Mel and I had got married the year before and we would have our first son, Will, a year later.

Four weeks previously, I had been working for Unilever, surrounded by bright and motivated people with all the perks you could wish for – pension scheme, career development, worldwide travel, training, personal mentors. On paper, it seemed an absurd thing to do, but I left this land of promise and opportunity after four and a half years, as much for my sanity as anything else. It was a top-class organization and for the rest of my working life, I would always start off any conversation about my career with a proud "My first few years were spent in brand management at Unilever …".

However, at that point in my life, Unilever was the wrong place for me. Being stuck in a big corporate cage was hurting too much.

I had just started a new job as a marketing trainer, working for a company called The Management Training Partnership (MTP) in "downtown" Aylesbury. I was on my own in the board room/meeting room/"somewhere quiet to work" room. There were only 20 other people or so employed by the company, and very few were in the office that day. In fact, very few had been in all week. No pension in place, no formal training, no clear career progression, no frills, no spills. The company turned over a couple of million or so and had been going for just seven or eight years. But MTP was pure heaven to me. The cat had finally got the cream.

I had joined a very small training company that designed, developed and delivered training courses in finance, marketing and interpersonal skills for a number of large global companies across the world, including, somewhat ironically, Unilever.

The reason I was so happy for the first time since leaving university was that I seemed to have found my perfect job. One that made me leap out of bed every morning. One I didn't mind putting in extra time for, and one that brought a big smile to my face whenever I talked about it with my friends. A job that would keep Worry and Winner happy for several years to come.

When I tried to identify the drivers underpinning my newly discovered joy, I could pinpoint two.

The first was the satisfaction I got from helping others develop and learn. I am more of a "people person" than a "task person", and this would remain my core motivational driver for the rest of my professional career. Let me explain further. When working as a brand manager in a large corporate organization, your main job objective is to grow brands profitably, and to do this you need to design products, develop advertising, produce business plans, etc. Your focus is always on tasks and getting "things" done. Yes, you work with or through people to achieve this, but fundamentally you are there to make money and keep the shareholders satisfied. As a result, my job at Unilever involved making daily decisions under the continual pressure of deadlines. These were often made based on my subjective opinion and I was always surrounded by other people, often more senior, whose subjective opinions were invariably stronger than mine. This fast-paced, commercially driven environment caused me stress because it was a mismatch with my core personality.

By contrast, when working as a trainer, the product *was* the people. The goal was to help a group of participants change the way they thought about something by connecting with them on a human and interpersonal level. What gave me enormous fulfilment was seeing people grow, have fun doing so, and then go on to do things differently as a result. This close alignment between the requirements of the job and my core motivations as a person meant I felt completely at home in this working environment. I was also surrounded by other like-minded people who shared the same preferences.

I was as happy as a pig in mud, a clam at high tide or a dog with two tails. Or, put another way, the shoes were a perfect fit, without a blister in sight.

INTROVERTS AND EXTROVERTS

The second reason for my joy was that the job fuelled my introverted nature. Introverts like to recharge their batteries by spending time alone, and they tend to lose energy from being around people for long periods. Warren Buffett, Bill Gates, J K Rowling, Barack Obama and Meryl Streep are all self-confessed introverts. Introverts often work slowly and deliberately. They like to focus on one task at a time, have impressive powers of concentration, but are also very happy to let their minds hibernate a little and wander a lot. Being deprived of sufficient mental space for "alone time" thinking or any physical space in which to disappear and recharge puts pressure on an introvert.

Extroverts, on the other hand, gain their energy from others and can find it diminishing when they spend too much time alone. They fill up their tanks by being social, and often find long periods of isolation exhausting and stressful. Muhammad Ali, Bill Clinton, Margaret Thatcher, Winston Churchill and Beyoncé are all famous extroverts. They tend to tackle assignments quickly, make fast decisions, and are comfortable multitasking and risk-taking. They love the buzz of a loud, busy working environment, relish seeing their diaries jam-packed with meetings, and positively purr when the corridors are congested with co-workers having conversations.

It's not completely binary though. A third personality type straddles the two and they are called ambiverts. They possess a balance of introvert and extrovert characteristics in approximately equal degrees. In the workplace, they treasure some time for personal reflection, but equally enjoy the buzz of group discussion. They are happy to join others for lunch in the office canteen, but equally happy to dine alone.

When I was working as a brand manager in Unilever, I was always the reluctant hub in a wheel full of spokes and it was very difficult to find the "me-time" I needed. I was perpetually on call and in demand. Being an introvert in a large extrovert-dominated company like Unilever caused me stress.

However, as a management trainer, the "extrovert time" I spent with people in the classroom – intense, exhilarating, and richly rewarding though it was – only worked because of the many gorgeous hours of solitude I enjoyed preparing for courses, and travelling to and from workshops. Bothered by nothing and nobody, my uncluttered mind felt liberated and free to be creative.

And, for what it's worth, I believe that the same principles around introversion, extroversion and ambiversion should also apply in your home life. For example, Mel is an extrovert. Her perfect weekend goes something like this: meal out with a group of friends on Friday evening, drinks party on Saturday, roast lunch with the whole family on Sunday. Shopping squeezed in sometime in between. Non-stop texting. Watching a period drama on Sunday evening with a glass of wine and a large pack of salt and vinegar crisps (cat and dog nearby). In bed at midnight after a final WhatsApp frenzy on one of her three girlfriend groups.

My ideal weekend is different. Meet up with a few close friends for drinks on either a Friday or Saturday, not both. Drink and chat from 6–8.30pm, by which time my social gene is exhausted. Rest of the weekend spent gardening, walking the dog, watching sport on TV. Alone obviously. My Sunday evening routine of choice consists of watching a one-hour documentary, followed by the news, 15 minutes in the bath listening to the radio, another 15 minutes tucked up reading a fast-moving thriller that doesn't require too much thinking. Lights out at 11pm. Pure heaven.

During the week, Mel and I have to negotiate hard about our weekend schedule to meet our respective extrovert and introvert needs. Fortunately for me, our cat, Maisie, and our dog, Peggy, offer to keep Mel close company which in turn takes the pressure off me. Thank God for pets.

To my way of thinking, whether you are an introvert, extrovert or ambivert, it's important to ensure both your working life and social life are in sync with your preferences.

If I am trying to alleviate stress at work, then the last thing I want to be doing is putting unnecessary pressure on my introversion by chit-chatting and partying non-stop over the weekend. The same principle applies for extroverts and ambiverts. Managing your mental health is a full-time job, which doesn't end on a Friday.

Pause for Thought

1. Do you feel you are an introvert, extrovert or ambivert? Is this based on self-perception or have you taken a personality assessment?
2. Depending on whether you are an introvert, extrovert or ambivert, does your current working environment support your personality type or not?
3. Which specific situations, interactions and activities, both at home and at work, boost your energy levels and which ones drain them?

Aged 30, I had found the right job, not only because my introverted nature and need for people focus were satisfied, but also because Winner and Worry were happy. Winner enjoyed an environment where I performed well, received positive feedback from co-workers, client and participants, and continued to learn and earn more. Equally importantly, Worry no longer had to deal with the daily stress of decision-making and having to tackle all the grey uncertainties of brand management. It was also a job that required meticulous preparation, a throwback to my school days. The world of training is more predictable, and the classroom has always been my refuge, a place where I feel most relaxed and in control of the situation.

Bizarrely enough, I was never adversely affected by the pressures of either training or facilitation. I think this is because these activities required me to be instinctive, to think on my feet. I didn't worry, not because I didn't care, but because there wasn't the time to overthink things or become anxious. This is why I find playing golf so much more stressful than rugby. The minutes spent walking from one shot to the next and the seconds spent standing over the ball just before I take the shot play havoc with my mind. My brain is bombarded by a dozen conflicting swing thoughts, all of which raise my stress levels and none of which have a positive effect on my golf swing.

Most of my 30s were a joyful time, both personally and professionally. When Emily was born, Will had just turned two and we were a proper little nuclear family. We had moved out of London and were enjoying the wide-open spaces of leafy Buckinghamshire.

I felt no more Sunday evening blues, no wishing the week away, and no longing for Friday to come round quickly. As a marketing trainer, I always dealt with professionals who had escaped the stresses and strains of office life, even if it was only for a couple of days or so. As a result, they were relaxed and easygoing, happy to let their hair down and have a bit of fun. I was only too eager to provide an environment where this was possible. I travelled the globe to far-off places, meeting all kinds of interesting people, learning loads, laughing lots. After five years of working there, I was promoted to become a Director of the company. I think it's safe to say, I was doing well. The freezer cabinet in the Birds Eye Wall's basement seemed a long, long time ago.

So, by all accounts, this chapter should now mark the end of a very short book with one straightforward moral: find a job you love and you will enjoy a life without stress. However, it doesn't end here because life always somehow manages to complicate things.

THE IMPORTANCE OF CAREER MOMENTUM

For many years, Johnnie Walker, the famous whisky brand, was supported by the advertising strapline – "Keep Walking". The insight was that if you got your head down and persevered, you would make progress. In 2015, it was felt that the work-oriented tone of the message didn't quite resonate in the way it used to. Genuine progress and meaningful success would only arrive if the starting point was a place of contentment. So, the brand changed tack and the new tagline became "Joy will take you further. Keep walking."

My problem, as I headed toward the end of my 30s, was that the joy of the job had started to wane. And this was affecting my joy of life. I had stopped walking.

In fact, the problem was Winner. He had become complacent, stopped growing professionally, settling for more of the same rather than experimenting with the new. My routine began to resemble a conveyor belt in a factory, churning out the same old stuff, day in, day out, going through the motions on autopilot – same training courses, same material, same old jokes. The net effect of this inertia was that I became slightly bored by the job and increasingly frustrated. I was not putting myself in situations that would stretch me and get the adrenaline going. I became stale.

Here's an interesting fact. Did you know that if a great white shark stops swimming, it stops receiving oxygen and dies? The reason for this is that, unlike other sharks, they don't have any buccal muscles. These muscles allow sharks to actively "inhale" water by using their cheek muscles to draw it into their mouth, which means they can stop moving but continue breathing. The great white shark doesn't have the luxury of buccal pumping. Instead, it relies on "obligate ram ventilation", a method of breathing that requires them to swim with their mouths wide open. The faster they swim, the more water is pushed through their gills, giving them the oxygen they require to survive. I was now a stuttering great white shark.

Although I had climbed the ranks in my company, this was not enough to satisfy Winner's hunger and his need to progress up the corporate ladder. The lack of prospects in a small company fuelled my sense of dissatisfaction and drove me to start looking at alternatives.

I was 37 years old. I had been with MTP for seven years and, overall, it had been a very rewarding period of my life. I had found the right career, but that career now needed fresh impetus. It had stalled and required an urgent kickstart. The previous April, our third child, Jack, was born. Will was now five years old and Emily, three. During this time, Mel and I had divided and conquered in terms of our overall responsibilities. In part, due to my excessive travelling, she happily sacrificed her career to take on the roles of full-time mum and domestic boss, overseeing all things financial and practical. This left me as the sole breadwinner in the family. The arrangement worked equally well for both of us, and we learned to adapt to a lifestyle that meant spending over 100 nights apart every year.

Our three young kids had never known anything different, but they would all understandably demand their share of "daddy time" whenever I was back in the country. But daddy was now sick and tired of getting on and off planes and, just as he had done seven years previously, it was time to make something happen and change tack.

A strong dose of something new was required to replace the mojo I had lost. I would receive it somewhat unexpectedly on a flight to New York in February of that year. It would be a lightning bolt, completely out of the blue.

HELP YOURSELF

TRY THE MATCHMAKER

The Matchmaker helps you align your values with your company's. The eight pairings outline the characteristics of any job. The more stars you get, the more aligned your needs are with those of the company. My one star out of eight for Birds Eye Wall's, in the example below, was not good enough.

Matchmaker – Me and Birds Eye Wall's

Highly structured *Birds Eye Wall's*	⟷	**Entrepreneurial** *Me*
Oriented toward individuals	⟷	**Team orientation** *Birds Eye Wall's, Me* ★
Driven by financials *Birds Eye Wall's*	⟷	**Driven by a higher purpose** *Me*
Focus on people development *Me*	⟷	**Focus on task completion** *Birds Eye Wall's*
Bias toward introverts *Me*	⟷	**Bias toward extroverts** *Birds Eye Wall's*
Logical and rational *Birds Eye Wall's*	⟷	**Creative and emotional** *Me*
Fast-paced decision-making *Birds Eye Wall's*	⟷	**Reflective and deliberate** *Me*
Work takes priority *Birds Eye Wall's*	⟷	**Work and life balance** *Me*

Working at MTP, I had five stars out of a possible eight, which meant that alignment between the company and me was much better. And the two dimensions that were most important to me – introvert versus extrovert, and people development versus task completion, both had stars against them. Good news!

Matchmaker – Me and MTP

Highly structured	**Entrepreneurial** *MTP, Me* ★
Oriented toward individuals *MTP*	**Team orientation** *Me*
Driven by financials *MTP*	**Driven by a higher purpose** *Me*
Focus on people development *MTP, Me* ★	**Focus on task completion**
Bias toward introverts *MTP, Me* ★	**Bias toward extroverts**
Logical and rational *MTP*	**Creative and emotional** *Me*
Fast-paced decision-making	**Reflective and deliberate** *MTP, Me* ★
Work takes priority	**Work and life balance** *MTP, Me* ★

WHAT TO DO

1. If your current job is causing you significant "bad" stress, use this framework to highlight the differences that exist between you and the company, dimension by dimension. Put your name and your company's name in the relevant boxes and insert a star where your names appear side by side.
2. Use the completed framework as the basis for a constructive conversation with your employers to see if you can achieve greater alignment. Be prepared to discuss the source(s) of your stress. Try to agree what your employers can do and what you can do.
3. Alternatively, if you are on the lookout for a new job, then use the dimensions of the Matchmaker to help you identify companies/positions where there is likely to be greater alignment between you and them.

A COUPLE OF WATCHOUTS

A. Try to identify one or two dimensions that are fundamental to your core values. In other words, what are your non-negotiables?
B. Ensure that you have enough "evidence" about both the company and yourself before placing any stars. If possible, ask a close co-worker for their unbiased views.

KEY TAKEAWAYS

- **Treat your job like a relationship:** If you want to better manage your stress, then it's important to view your time in the workplace in the same way you would view any two-way relationship.
- **Seek alignment between your personality preferences and your career:** You have needs based on your own motivations, and the company you work for will also have its own. Ensure they are aligned as closely as possible, but remember that the company is always likely to be the dominant partner. Fit is everything.
- **Enjoying work is good for your mental health:** Your career might be a rollercoaster and there will be plenty of bumps along the way. You won't enjoy every job that you do, but if you have the opportunity, try not to settle for second or third best. Life's too short.

3

DRIP, DRIP, DRIP, DRIP

Minimize the destructive impact of "bad"
stress at work

The never-ending drizzle of stress is unfortunately part and parcel of life in many corporate environments. It's undoubtedly the scourge of the modern workplace. This chapter will focus on the destructive impact it can have, especially when you find yourself stuck in a job for which you are ill-equipped. There will be four themes:

1. **Fishing in the wrong ponds:** Experiencing stress by doing a job that presents a fundamental mismatch with your core personality.
2. **Running on empty:** Neglecting to look after the basic needs of your mind and body – food, sleep, exercise, socializing – as the pressure mounts.
3. **Missing the warning signs:** Being oblivious to the mounting evidence that things are not right.
4. **Keeping the silence:** Being fearful of opening up to family, friends and co-workers about your deteriorating mental state.

Before we get stuck into the chapter, let's discuss irritating sounds.

STRESS DROPS KEEP FALLIN' ON MY HEAD

A study was conducted in 2016 involving 2,000 people to find out the most annoying everyday noises. These were the top five:

1. Snoring
2. Loud chewing
3. A dog barking
4. Fingernails running down a chalkboard
5. Loud slurping of tea or coffee

There were some quite amusing entries further down the list: "People kissing loudly" came in at number 25, the "Crazy Frog Song" was at 26 and "loud yawns" made the chart at 40.

"Worry is like a rocking chair; it gives you something to do but never gets you anywhere."

Erma Bombeck, humorist

What's interesting is that there is a biological explanation for the discomfort you experience when you are subjected to these irritating sounds. Researchers have found that the section of the brain that regulates emotions, the amygdala, takes over the hearing part of the brain when a noise starts to grate. It sends a "distress signal" to the auditory cortex, and the higher the frequency, the more "distressing" the signal is.

The noise that irritates me most comes in at number 16: dripping taps. Particularly in the dead of night when I'm in between the conscious and unconscious. Taken in isolation, one drip is not particularly bothersome, but over time, the metronomic nature of drip, drip, drip, drip begins to have an increasingly adverse effect on me. The noise seems to become louder and louder, and my discomfort is caused as much by the anticipation of the next drop as it is by the sound of the drop itself.

"Dripping tap syndrome" is a powerful metaphor for the impact of stress on the human brain. You start off not feeling much discomfort, then little things begin to irritate and apply pressure in different places.

- Drip ... nothing too painful, but persistent nonetheless.
- Drip ... drip ... soldier on, this will pass. Pressure builds.
- Drip ... drip ... drip ... things become more and more uncomfortable. You feel trapped and slightly claustrophobic.
- Drip ... drip ... drip ... drip ... More pressure. Is it imagined or real? Doesn't matter, either way you still feel trapped. Then one day, without warning, the flood gates open.

FISHING IN THE WRONG PONDS

There can be little doubt that human beings were not designed to spend too much time in aircraft cabins. Constipation. Bad breath. Ruined taste buds. Popping ears. Swollen legs. Blood clots. Dizziness. Dry skin. Flatulence. Increased tension, anxiety and stress. These are some of the physical and mental symptoms that, according to medical research, can affect individuals flying long haul at high altitudes. Doesn't sound like much fun, does it?

But for much of my 30s I loved it. Although I wasn't immune to several of the unpleasant conditions listed above, this time was pure gold dust to me. Client-paid business trips to the Far East and the Americas were sacred pockets of peace and calm. My mind always seemed able to declutter itself quickly and remain as clear as a bell high above the clouds. The eight, nine, ten or more hours of "me-time" available, uninterrupted by emails pinging into my inbox, presented me with the opportunity to do much of my "big thinking". With an absence of hustle and bustle, Worry always felt wonderfully relaxed, and Winner was allowed to let his creative juices flow freely, with time aplenty for plotting and planning. Pure paradise.

It was in this land of hope and possibility that I was flying to the US with my Unilever client, Andy Bird, to persuade the Americans to embrace the company's flagship Foundation training programme for marketing graduates.

I was 38 years old and had been working with Andy for about two years. He was a bright and gifted individual with a First-Class Honours degree from Oxford, backed up by an impressive track record working for Unilever in the UK, India and Singapore in a variety of strategic marketing roles over a number of years. His latest position was Vice President of Unilever's Global Marketing Academy, where he had spent the last four years driving the development of Unilever's corporate marketing capabilities – a groundbreaking initiative that he had been handpicked to lead. Andy was a class act who made everything look easy. On top of all that, he was a personable guy with whom I had a lot in common.

We had both reached that "So now what …?" stage in our respective careers, and we got talking about important stuff …

Helped partly by the courage of drink and the clarity of altitude, we started mulling over our respective plans for the future. For some time now, I had been looking to leave MTP where I'd spent the last eight years. I had become increasingly frustrated by the lack of prospects and progress, and had been suffering from itchy feet for a couple of years.

Having made a great success as head of the Marketing Academy, Andy was also looking for his next move in the training/learning/capability arena. He was an ambitious individual too.

WAS MARK VENTURING
TOO CLOSE TO THE SUN?

After a few tentative "how abouts" and "what ifs", we nudged our way toward the exciting possibility of going into business together. The Big Idea was to combine best practice in brand marketing with leading-edge learning in order to improve the skills of managers working in large organizations. It seemed an obvious idea when we added up our respective experience and expertise.

Unfortunately, Worry remained in deep hibernation throughout the trip, oblivious to the plot that was unfolding.

When I woke up the next morning in New York, I felt like a mischievous schoolboy who had done something he really shouldn't have. The night before, we had engaged in a "big" conversation that could have serious consequences for both of us. Very sensibly, Andy and I agreed to sleep on the idea for a couple of days, giving us both time and space to find out whether the gin and tonics had clouded our better judgement. I was convinced they hadn't. Winner was too. We had both taken our chances high above the Atlantic Ocean and something exciting had emerged.

A few days later, when we got in touch back in the UK, we still thought it was an idea that merited further consideration. During the call, Andy mentioned that he had been working with somebody he rated highly, an independent consultant called Mhairi McEwan. Mhairi had also started her career at Unilever, where she spent 13 years rising through the marketing ranks, working in the UK, France and Egypt. She became Vice President Marketing (Europe) for Pepsico International and Walkers Foods before becoming a successful consultant working for companies like Unilever, Diageo and Burger King. Mhairi was likeable, extremely commercial and, as it turned out, well-connected in the business world. Another class act.

Since our trip to the US, Andy had contacted Mhairi to gauge her interest, and she was really excited by the potential of the idea. We suggested meeting at the Runnymede Hotel in Egham to introduce ourselves properly, discuss the new business idea in greater depth and work out how we could make this all happen.

When I left the hotel after two electrifying hours, my head was spinning, the new idea was quickly gaining weight and momentum. The power of that idea, the foundation upon which the business grew quickly, was such that 17 years later the company would be purchased by Accenture for many millions of pounds.

"An invasion of armies can be resisted, but not an idea whose time has come."

Victor Hugo, poet

The wheels were in motion the moment each of us stepped outside the Runnymede Hotel that day. I resigned from my company a month or so later. During my three-month notice period, all my mental energy was channelled toward the new venture and the three of us were soon up and running at full pelt. All systems were go.

In those first few months after the Runnymede meeting, the three of us would meet regularly to discuss, debate and agree the strategic direction the new business would take and all the usual hurdles any new company would need to consider. Which companies are we going to target? How will we position ourselves in the market and differentiate our offering from the competition? How are we going to price our services? Will we take on full-time employees or use freelance consultants? How much should we pay them and ourselves? Ironically, the company name turned out to be one of the easiest things to pick: Brand Learning. It embodied our positioning perfectly.

The company was officially founded and incorporated in July of that year. The three of us were equal shareholders. A new and exciting chapter was quickly unfolding in all our lives.

In no time at all, we were a proper little entity going from strength to strength. From the word go we needed to agree who did what as far as the running and management of the company was concerned. Who would look after the administration and the back office, the finances, the legal stuff? Who would establish human resource policies? Which of us was best qualified to drive the development of the website? This workload needed to be shared out equally between the three of us so that we could divide in order to conquer.

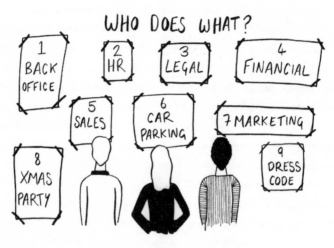

WHO DOES WHAT?

IF ONLY MARK HAD PICKED
6, 8 AND 9

Without thinking too hard, I offered to work alongside our professional advisors to manage our accounts and look after our legal affairs as Company Secretary. In hindsight, this was a big and naive mistake. Although I was fairly comfortable with the theory of the balance sheet, cash flow, and profit and loss statements, the responsibility for overseeing the finances of the fast-growing business would prove to be one of the straws that broke this camel's back. I soon became blinded by numbers, numbers, numbers.

The legal stuff wasn't much better – Memorandum and Articles of Association, Service Agreements, Event of Default, Option Period, Transfer Terms. All I remember from my stint as a "trainee lawyer" was trying to make sense of these alien terms, deciphering a language that never seemed to be written in plain English. Even though it was basic contractual stuff, and even though my "hand was being held" by the experts, it was still mumbo-jumbo to me.

One of my most important duties during the set-up was leading the development of the Shareholders' Agreement, the document laying out the various intricacies around our share ownership. Much of this focused on what would occur if one of the shareholders were to leave the business prematurely, what would happen to their shares, and how those shares would then be valued. I dithered and dallied to such an extent that we never did get around to signing it.

Ironically, many years later, that very same unsigned document would emerge from the shadows of my attic with a very painful sting in its tale. More about that later.

No doubt about it, I had jumped into the wrong pond. I was a "concepts and clouds" type, much more into the touchy-feely, and here I was volunteering to take charge of two areas of the business that were the complete opposite, the crunchy and the clinical. Back in my early 30s, I had already established I was a "people focus" rather than a "task completion" kind of guy. My short stint in brand management at Unilever had taught me that valuable lesson. And the mojo I had rediscovered when I kickstarted my training career at MTP had reconfirmed this. What was I thinking?

Drip.

Pause for Thought

1. Are you currently in a role that is aligned with your personal and professional strengths and competencies?
2. If not, can you identify where the misalignment lies?
3. What are you able to do to correct this?

RUNNING ON AN EMPTY TANK

We were coming toward the end of the year. The planning period for the new company had taken place between the Runnymede meeting in April and November when we officially began trading. During that time, I had also been working out my notice period at MTP. I didn't have the luxury of any gardening leave or two-week holiday in the sun to recharge my batteries. By the time we kicked things off, I was pretty exhausted.

"He felt like an old sponge steeped in paraffin and left in the sun to dry."

Douglas Adams, author

Mhairi, Andy and I now had day and night jobs. My day job was a marketing trainer. I was still travelling to the US and Japan, running five-day workshops, and spending weeks away from home. I had been globetrotting for the last nine years, and the glamour of foreign travel had gradually worn off. An Inter-Continental hotel looks more or less the same in New York as it does in Tokyo, and airports are airports the world over. I felt stale and washed-out. The luxury of client-paid business-class travel was always a bonus, but this ringfenced time for creative thinking, munching peanuts and watching films had now sadly given way to checking financial spreadsheets and proofreading legal documents. My night job.

Drip, drip.

When starting your own business, you quickly realize how much you miss the little things you took for granted in a larger organization with more resources. In that cosy and protected environment, you are blessed with assistants to help you prepare presentations and sort out travel arrangements, the IT team are only ever one phone call away from coming to your rescue; the finance department is always on hand to process your expenses and pay you on time. These luxuries were no longer available to me. It was now do-it-yourself.

Along with my two partners, I also spent a painful day finding out all I needed to know about Excel to improve the bookkeeping skills I required to carry out my financial role. And the task of developing my non-existent capabilities in PowerPoint became another urgent "must learn item" on my ever growing to-do list.

Accountant, lawyer, Microsoft Office expert, secretary, international management trainer. Five in one. Although each of these "jobs" didn't present insurmountable challenges on their own, it was tackling them all at the same time that caused me mental anguish. And when your tank is running on empty, you don't have either the strength or the stamina to stretch yourself in new directions that require sharpness of mind.

MENTAL HEALTH FACTS

242 entrepreneurs and 93 demographically matched comparison participants took part in an anonymous online self-report study. Findings included:

- Self-reported mental health concerns present across 72% of the entrepreneurs. The corresponding figure for the comparison participants was 49%.
- Groups did not differ in terms of anxiety, with 27% of entrepreneurs and 26% of non-entrepreneurs reporting anxiety concerns.

Source: Are entrepreneurs "touched with fire"? University of California San Francisco study

As far as Worry was concerned, there was just too much uncertainty, and too many things to get my head around at once. The only time I stopped worrying was when I stepped into the training room in either London, New York or Tokyo. That always remained my sanctuary, my safe place, where I felt in control, where I enjoyed helping other people learn and develop themselves. This was the very core of my personality, and it was being badly shaken now that I was stepping outside my comfort zone.

Drip, drip, drip.

In combination, all of the above became very challenging and none of it was particularly enjoyable. And the pressure I placed on myself to keep up with both Andy and Mhairi, who as far as I could tell seemed to be coping effortlessly with their equally heavy workloads, only served to raise my stress levels. They made everything look so easy and, despite my best efforts, I was developing a nagging feeling that I wasn't quite pulling my weight.

Somewhat ominously, I was also starting to get the dreaded "Sunday night blues", something I had not expected when I took the plunge into the exciting world of entrepreneurship. The last time I had experienced "Monday fright" was during my Unilever days, ten years previously.

Drip, drip, drip, drip.

The first ten months since the Runnymede meeting had certainly been an exhilarating ride, but it had begun to take its toll on me both physically and mentally. Stress was back in town, but it wasn't pushing me on to reach further or work harder. It didn't leave me feeling energized and uplifted. That would have been "good" stress. No, the unrelenting pressure had teamed up with the lack of enjoyment, and this mix had led to an emotional pain that was becoming chronic. This was "bad" stress in action, and my genetic make-up was starting to moan and groan.

Pause for Thought

1. Are you experiencing either "good" or "bad" stress in your current role? How do these manifest themselves for you both physically and emotionally?
2. If you had to rank your current resilience levels when managing stress (1 = very poor, 10 = stellar), where would you fall on that scale as of today?
3. What are you doing to strengthen your levels of resilience? Are there any specific actions you can take to improve this?

MISSING THE WARNING SIGNS

Although Winner was huffing and puffing like a boxer going through a tough few rounds, he was still insistent that this discomfort was the price of success. He would reassure me with the following rallying cry: "Mark, you're not an entrepreneur until you have had your first breakdown." Worry would simply nod incredulously, wearing those smug "I told you so" looks and that "Maybe I should have been properly consulted when we embarked on this little venture" expression.

"If you have one passion in life – football – and you pursue it to the exclusion of everything else, it becomes very dangerous."

Eric Cantona, soccer player

Winner kept his head down, somewhat sheepishly. He would have benefited greatly from work carried out by Robert J Vallerand, the Canadian Professor of Psychology, who explained the difference between Obsessive Passion (OP) and Harmonious Passion (HP). OP occurs when you begin to relentlessly pursue the one thing you are passionate about, at the expense of everything around you. This passion can become all-consuming, overpowering and, like a drug, you begin to rely on it to build your self-worth and self-esteem. If left unchecked, it can lead to burnout. HP on the other hand occurs when you become immersed in the task for the pleasure of the task itself. This "flow state" means that you can remain totally absorbed by what you are doing without losing perspective of the bigger picture. You retain the ability to enjoy multiple areas of interest and they all collaborate harmoniously for the benefit of the whole being. No doubt about it, I was experiencing OP.

Small cracks were starting to appear – sleeping badly, eating less, worrying more, laughing rarely. Socializing with friends had been put on the back-burner, and stress-reducing physical activity had become a long-forgotten luxury. I was too preoccupied with negative thoughts to relax properly, and the less I was able to relax, the more preoccupied I became.

Drip, drip, drip, drip, drip.

A side effect of my deteriorating state was that I was becoming increasingly indecisive. Decisions that should have been straightforward were suddenly difficult to make, and everything seemed to take longer to process and complete. My head was crammed full of so many pressing jobs that my mental machinery was starting to seize up.

Suddenly, I was having menacing flashbacks to the basement wandering at Birds Eye Wall's. The symptoms were worryingly familiar – confusion, moments of fear, little signs of panic, increasing levels of agitation and anxiety, as well as a feeling of complete isolation.

Twelve months after that life-changing trip with Andy to the US, I was back on the plane to New York to run another five-day workshop with Unilever. This time I didn't feel quite so liberated by the magical effect of altitude.

Hypoxia is a condition in which the body is deprived of adequate oxygen supply at the tissue level. It is thought to be the reason why people become emotional when watching sentimental movies mid-flight. I was sitting by a window, staring out of it so that nobody could see I was crying. I was crying because I was frightened. I was frightened because I was unsure whether I had the right kind of visa to enter the US. I had terrifying visions of being denied entry at the border and having to return to the UK. How would I explain my "irresponsible" actions to the client? What excuses for my "incompetence" would I offer to Andy and Mhairi?

The tears, the fears and the terror were very real, but they were completely out of proportion with the issue at hand. Needless to say, the whole thing turned out to be a non-issue and I was admitted into the US without a problem, but the root cause of my extreme stress had nothing to do with visas. What I was doing was catastrophizing or, in medical jargon, experiencing a "cognitive distortion". This happens when a person predicts an unfavourable outcome to an event and then decides that if this outcome does happen, the results will be disastrous; 99 times out of 100, the prediction never materializes.

One could argue that catastrophizing has its upsides. After all, it means that you never end up being disappointed when bad things do happen. However, this pattern of thinking can be very destructive, because unnecessary and persistent worrying can lead to poor self-esteem, cycles of low mood, even anxiety and depression. And it can become a self-fulfilling prophecy. The more negative thoughts you have, the more your stress hormones like cortisol are spiked, and the less likely you will be able to think and act clearly. Then things will almost certainly go wrong.

Catastrophizing can also be a clear sign that you are already mentally unwell. This was the case with me.

Drip, drip, drip, drip, drip, drip.

Pause for Thought

1. If you experience chronic stress, can you pinpoint the "early warning signs" before you might hit your tipping point? What do these look like emotionally and physically?
2. In your immediate circles, can you identify somebody who knows you as well as you know yourself, who can give you a tap on the shoulder if you are about to go over the cliff edge?
3. Have they been briefed on your "early warning system"? Do they know which signs to look out for?

KEEPING THE SILENCE

Throughout this difficult period, I felt unable to confide in Andy and Mhairi. In retrospect, this decision not to open up was a bad error of judgement, and for all the wrong reasons.

Firstly, I didn't know either of them very well at a personal level, and divulging something this sensitive seemed out of the question. What exactly would I say? "Listen, I am sorry to bother you both, but I think I am having a nervous breakdown. How are you both doing?" In the last few years, great strides have been taken to destigmatize mental illness in the workplace, but back then it was a taboo subject with very little guidance on what to say or do for all parties concerned.

"I have learned now that while those who speak out about one's miseries usually hurt, those who keep silence hurt more."

C.S. Lewis, writer and lay theologian

Secondly, I kept trying to tell myself that the discomfort I was feeling was perfectly normal. At least, this is what Winner kept insisting. Things would get easier sooner or later and I just had to ride out the storm. In any case, most of my friends were under some kind of pressure as they tried to forge ahead in their respective careers. My situation was certainly not unique.

Thirdly, I had spent the last year or so waiting patiently for this big opportunity to arrive. The last thing I was going to do was jeopardize it by admitting to either of my partners that I was in any kind of trouble. I had placed such great expectations on myself and had pinned all my highest of hopes on the success of this venture, I just wasn't prepared to dampen them right then. I felt like one of those proud boxers who just can't bring himself to admit to his corner that he is now hurting all over, that he has perhaps bitten off more than he can chew, and that maybe it's time to throw in the towel.

Not only was I feeling under increasing pressure at work, but I was also beginning to detach myself from any meaningful

EMILY'S STORY

The pain of silence

Three years ago, I had just started working as a studio runner at ITV. However, I began the job still in the grip of anorexia nervosa, a mental illness. I was a "functioning anorexic". In simple terms, this means that although I looked well on the outside, I was still using my eating disorder as an invisible crutch – counting calories, restricting my diet and hiding my struggles from everybody.

My working hours were unpredictable and long. Coping is hard enough for a healthy person, let alone somebody who is on the edge both physically and mentally. The job became more stressful and, after weeks of steady decline, I came to a crossroads – either continue to suffer in silence or come clean to my boss, Susie. I chose the latter and it was the best decision I have ever made.

The instant relief I felt was immense. A weight had been lifted off my shoulders. Susie's reaction was incredible. She sent me straight home where I remained for two weeks on sick leave. With my permission, she explained to the other runners what had been going on. I have since learned that my co-workers had noticed my downward spiral, but were simply too nervous to say anything that might upset me. I've realized over the years that saying anything to someone struggling – a simple "How are you?" or "Are you ok?" – is better than staying silent.

On my return, Susie had rescheduled my working week to suit my recovery and booked in regular "check-up chats" to see how I was getting on. My friends at work were also on hand if I needed to swap a shift or take a meal break. I will always be grateful to Susie and the team.

kind of social life. And whenever I did go out with friends or family, I was only ever "out" in the physical sense of the word. Mentally, I always stayed in my own little world, cogitating and ruminating.

It was even worse with the children. I can vividly remember apologizing to Will, my eldest son, who was now six and Emily who was four, trying to explain what I was doing, why I was abroad so often, and why, even when I was back home, I was spending so much time in my office. I promised them we would hopefully soon be spending much more time together. I felt extremely guilty about not being a proper dad and not being there for them, but as I made my excuses, they just looked at me blankly, too young to really understand the inner turmoil their father was experiencing.

Drip, drip, drip, drip, drip, drip, drip.

The drips were becoming too persistent. They were now making too much noise in my head and were beginning to hurt. It was time to see the doctor. The last time I'd been to see a doctor about my state of mind was back in my Unilever days following the basement episode. Ominously, the same symptoms were beginning to align, so I decided to make an appointment. Worry had begun to nag me like a mother hen, urging me to get help as quickly as possible.

I explained to the doctor that there was really nothing to panic about, that I was just feeling a bit anxious, not sleeping terribly well. I was trying to convince myself as much as him that I was simply taking preventative measures to nip things in the bud. Better safe now than sorry later.

I was prescribed 5mg of chlordiazepoxide, a medication for anxiety disorders. I also agreed to visit the Dove Centre, a counselling unit in Aylesbury to pick up some tips on how to cope with the escalating stress. I took the pills daily, heeded the advice given, and every morning woke up in the hope that everything would magically be better. Wishful thinking.

I became a sucker for self-help books and dived into *Don't Sweat the Small Stuff*, a seminal book written by Richard Carlson. It contained a myriad of tips, all of which made eminent sense: "Make peace with imperfection"; "Think of your problems as potential teachers"; "When our attention is in the present moment, we push fear from our minds". They were great soundbites which I devoured with the same relish I might consume canapés at a fancy party. In both cases, they fill you up but always leave you wanting more. They were never quite enough.

Unfortunately, I had gone past the tipping point. The tablets, the self-help books and the counselling were the equivalent of trying to extinguish a raging fire with a child's toy water pistol. All the structural damage had already been done to my brain. The neurotransmitters had long stopped talking coherently to one another. I stumbled on for the next few weeks, barely functioning, and life was very painful.

Then, one day the floodgates opened. Mixing my metaphors, the last few months had been a death by a thousand drips.

Pause for Thought

1. Are you feeling ashamed about the state of your mental health and worried about discussing it with others?
2. In specific terms, what worries you most about confiding in someone?
3. Which person, in either your personal or professional circles, do you think would show most empathy? How might you best approach this person?

HELP YOURSELF

TAKE THE STRESS TEST

I've rewound the clock and completed the questions below based on how I was feeling about six months into the new venture, indicating what, in hindsight, I should have done.

STRESS TEST 1			
To what extent would you say that your personality traits were aligned with the work you are currently doing?			
Not at all	Not very much	Well enough	Totally
X (legal and financial role)			
Actions: I should have had a conversation with my two partners quickly and agreed to take on a different managerial role in the start-up that was more in my comfort zone.			

STRESS TEST 2

At this moment in time, how full is your resilience tank?

Empty	Quarter	Three-quarters	Full
	X		

Actions: I should have started a daily routine of exercise, and been more disciplined about separating work from play.

STRESS TEST 3

Do you have an early warning system in place for when things get tough?

Nothing at all	A few measures	Fully operational
	X	

Action: I should have had a proper conversation with my wife about the role she could play, encouraging her to raise the red flag as soon as she became concerned.

STRESS TEST 4

How likely are you to open up to others about your mental health struggles?

Highly unlikely	Maybe	Very likely
X		

Actions: I should have talked to my two partners about the stress I felt under, been more open with close friends and family, and got checked out by a medical professional sooner.

WHAT TO DO

1. When considering your current job, answer each of the Stress Test questions as honestly as possible.
2. Depending on how you answered each question, identify one or more actions that you intend to take in order to migrate toward the right-hand side of the box.

3. Ask a close friend, co-worker or family member to act as a sounding board and provide you with honest and constructive feedback.

A COUPLE OF WATCHOUTS

A. It is definitely worth taking the Stress Test even if you are not feeling stressed in the workplace at the moment. Metaphorically speaking, it's prudent to check over the car, even when it's running smoothly.

B. If you do find yourself putting an X mainly in the left-hand box, it's even more important to be both decisive and proactive as far as taking action is concerned.

KEY TAKEAWAYS

- **Fish in the right career ponds:** The more aligned your personality traits are with the work you are currently doing, the better chance you have of avoiding stress that might be damaging to you.
- **Run on a full tank:** If you find yourself in any kind of demanding job, it's important that you discipline yourself to keep your resilience tank as full as possible by exercising, eating and sleeping well and socializing enough.
- **Build an early warning system:** Ensure that you have clearly identified those early signals that indicate you might be sliding down the slippery path. It's also important that a close friend or family member has your back.
- **Break the silence:** It's far better if you can find the courage to open up to friends, family and co-workers about how you are feeling – sooner rather than later.

4

THE UNSETTLED MIND

Understand how a stress-related nervous breakdown feels

The wheels had come off the bus. "Good" stress had turned to "bad" stress and things had become ugly. In the next two chapters, I will describe in detail how my mental state deteriorated rapidly, taking me down dark alleyways. The "bad" stress would lead to a breakdown, which would in turn develop into full-blown agitated depression. I was entering uncharted territory and it was going to be a very frightening  experience, not just for me but for my whole family.

In this chapter, I will cover the following themes:

1. **The dissection of a nervous breakdown:** This term is commonly thrown around, but what exactly is it? What does one look like in the flesh?

2. **The irrational language of mental ill health:** What does it feel like to experience a condition called agitated depression? What thoughts were flooding through my head? How could I explain my erratic behaviours to myself and others? What was the best way for others to communicate with me?
3. **Sources of help and support:** Who and what do you turn to in order to help you best manage your agitated depression?

For people who have never experienced depression first-hand, it might seem a mystery. The lack of physical symptoms makes it difficult to understand exactly how it feels, and it can be challenging for those who have experienced it to find suitable words to describe it. This is how two famous, erudite people, blessed with the gift of prose, summed it up.

First up is Stephen Fry, English comedian, actor and author: "If you know someone who's depressed, please resolve never to ask them why. Depression isn't a straightforward response to a bad situation; depression just is, like the weather. Try to understand the blackness, lethargy, hopelessness and loneliness they're going through. Be there for them when they come through the other side. It's hard to be a friend to someone who's depressed, but it's one of the kindest, noblest and best things you will ever do."

J K Rowling next: "Depression is the most unpleasant thing I have experienced. It's that absence of being able to envisage that you will ever be cheerful again. The absence of hope. That very deadened feeling, which is so different from feeling sad. Sad hurts but it's a healthy feeling. It's a necessary thing to feel. Depression is very different."

A NERVOUS BREAKDOWN

It was 9 April, just another Monday morning, when I entered my home office at around 8am. I sat at my desk, switched on my PC, then opened up my notebook and had a quick look at my to-do list. I turned to the first item. My mind was in a frenzy and I found it impossible to focus on the task I had begun. I tried again, but still no luck. I was unable to concentrate for more than a few seconds before my mind became distracted, invaded by the other items on my list, all screaming for my attention. After 30 minutes of wasted time, spent either staring aimlessly at my computer screen or pacing up and down the room, desperately trying to make sense of what was happening, I needed to break the circuit.

Let's grab a cup of coffee. Deep breath. Nothing serious.

> *"One of the symptoms of an approaching nervous breakdown is the belief that one's work is terribly important."*
>
> Bertrand Russell, polymath

I was back at my desk 20 minutes later, attempting to tackle another task on the list. It wasn't a particularly challenging one, but this made no difference. I was unable to complete the job at hand. I was starting to become more and more agitated. I knew the longer I sat there not doing anything, the less time I would have to complete everything I had to do. The pressure continued to build. Very briefly, I managed to pull myself together, remembering what the local counselling unit had told me about coping with stress. Deep breathing was the trick, particularly if it came all the way from the body's dominant breathing muscle – the diaphragm. During stressful moments, the conscious act of taking long, slow and deep breaths from the belly could help reduce tightness. Chest breathing wasn't any good because it made the body tense, increasing stress and feelings of anxiety.

Close your eyes ... breathe in, hold your breath, breathe out ... breathe in, hold your breath, breathe out ... breathe in, hold your breath, breathe out ...

That morning, I was as tight as a coiled spring. I was finding it difficult enough breathing through my mouth, let alone from my chest or my belly.

Five minutes later, I was back at my computer. This time, surely. Unfortunately not. My mind was still racing. I completed a few more frantic circuits of the room. I began to bang my head hard against the wall out of sheer frustration. I did this several times in a futile attempt to knock some sense into me. This wasn't happening, I told myself. This couldn't be happening. It was now mid-morning, time was marching on, and I had been totally unproductive for about two hours. My stress levels were rising with every passing minute. Nothing had been ticked off my to-do list.

I left my home office again and returned to the kitchen. I needed to talk to Mel who had dropped the two older children off at school. By explaining my problem slowly and calmly, I tried to normalize the situation, make out things were not as serious as they so obviously were. Mel suggested I reduce my list for the day to a couple of items only and tackle them one at a time. As usual, Mel's rational advice seemed very sound and sensible. Of course, I told myself, that was the obvious thing to do. Silly me. Reduce the length of the list, take one thing at a time, get some momentum going and once you are in the groove, you'll be fine. Back to normal.

I returned to my office desperately hoping the little blip was just that. I pretended I was starting the day afresh, but back at my desk, all was unfortunately not okay. I picked one thing to focus on, just like Mel had suggested. But still nothing doing. Mind frozen. The computer had now turned into a man-eating lion, not allowing me anywhere near the keyboard, roaring at me to go away and not come back.

Another chat with Mel. With increasing panic, we made an emergency appointment at the surgery, and 30 minutes later we were there explaining to the doctor the events of the morning, in the context of the last couple of months. Without hesitation, he decided my medication needed changing but also recommended I took time off work. He suggested three weeks.

Pause for Thought

1. Have you ever had feelings of panic at work? If so, why and how often have these occurred?
2. If you have experienced high levels of stress or panic at work, what impact did this have on your job performance? What did this look like?
3. What, if any, were the after-effects of this stress? For example, did it affect your sleeping, eating and socializing patterns? If so, how?

As soon as he uttered those magical words, "time off work", I felt this enormous sense of relief. The burden was lifted. Yes, I knew this would have implications all round, but the situation had been taken out of my hands. The doctor reassured me this was not unusual. I had simply experienced burnout, which was quite common and nothing a few weeks' rest wouldn't help. I made a difficult call to Andy, who was unsurprisingly shocked and sympathetic in equal measures. This had come completely out of the blue for both of my partners. Up to this point, I had been functioning "normally" in the eyes of the outside world. But inside I had obviously been close to breaking point, and my brain had now decided to call it a day.

STEPPING OFF THE PAINFUL TREADMILL

For the next three weeks, I remained at home on sick leave, under strict instructions not to think about work and not to go anywhere near my home office. The last one was easy enough to comply with, but it certainly wasn't a relaxing time or the much-needed break that would help restart the engine and put me back on track.

Unfortunately, much of it was spent coming to terms with what had happened. My mind was still whirring away, day and night. It was taking part in the 24-hour Le Mans race where there are no pit stops and you just go round and round the same track. Time after time after time. Mel and I tried to socialize a bit, pretending everything was normal, but it wasn't. We both knew it. My conversations both with her and our friends were distant and detached.

Winner was in denial and kept trying to persuade me this was just a tiny inconvenience all budding entrepreneurs experienced. Worry had started battening down the hatches, getting himself ready for an impending storm.

On Friday 27 April, I met my two partners at the end of the three-week break to decide a way forward. We met in a restaurant in London to talk things over, and there was plenty of sympathy and reassuring noises. I was honest with them about the pressure I had been feeling during the last few weeks. I wasn't coping and needed to put the brakes on for a bit. As a result, I was relieved of my financial accountant's responsibilities.

No more numbers.

From that point on, Mhairi would take control of all things financial and legal, and she proved to be much better qualified than me in both areas. And when she recruited an accountant with 40 years' experience, the commercial side of the business would finally be run by able professionals rather than by a willing but unskilled amateur, out of his depth.

My overall workload was reduced, and an ongoing plan of attack was agreed to help get me moving in the right direction again. A return to work on Monday. Normality resumed. It didn't quite feel that way over the next 48 hours. The gradual build-up of pressure in my mind through Saturday and Sunday were scant evidence of any return to normality. The Le Mans race was still going strong in my head.

THE SCARY MOMENT OF BREAKDOWN

Monday morning. A restless night's sleep. I walked into my home office like a man entering a room where he knows he won't be welcome. I opened my workbook and looked at my much reduced to-do list, but each item still seemed like the equivalent of climbing Everest. As my computer booted up slowly, I was praying it would be less hostile than it had been three weeks previously.

It wasn't. Once again, my mind seized up.

No! No! No! No! No! Noooooo! Please God, no!

More pacing up and down, more demented headbanging, more futile deep breathing. But nothing had changed. Nothing had worked – the stronger medication, the three-week break, the reduced responsibilities had had no positive effect whatsoever. The little blip had just become a big one. The engine had been spluttering badly for a number of months. I hadn't got it checked over when I should have, and now it had given up the ghost. A few frantic attempts to turn on the ignition, but it was stone dead.

Here's the irony. Although a nervous breakdown is extremely frightening, I have come to the conclusion that it's probably an essential part of your human defence system. If you put your hand on a hot oven plate by accident, the moment your mind senses you'll get burnt, you instinctively pull it away to avoid it getting hurt. Similarly, if you try to hold your breath under water for a long period of time, your mind orders you to resurface when your brain is being deprived of the oxygen it needs.

When stress builds up to a point where things are becoming psychologically and physically dangerous, the brain simply takes matters out of your hands. It presses the emergency "stop" button, shutting you and your system down whether you like it or not. It won't restart the engine until it thinks it's safe to do so. In most cases, this takes place relatively quickly, once it's absolutely sure you are out of danger. This is what had happened to me many years previously when I had experienced my panic attack at Birds Eye Wall's. This time around, my engine would need major repair work and my brain wouldn't open up for business anytime soon.

A "nervous breakdown" is not a diagnostic term, and you won't find a scientific definition in any mental health professional's lexicon. An "adjustment disorder" is as close as you will get diagnostically. "Nervous" or "mental" breakdowns are purely layman's terms to describe the point when you are unable to cope with life anymore and you come to a grinding halt.

MARY'S STORY

I just couldn't stop myself from crying

I was HR Director at a global food company. I was hardworking and well respected so when I was offered an expansion to my role I saw it as further validation of my position and my success. However, it virtually doubled my workload overnight and increased my exposure to a number of tricky conflicts. I felt as though I was in a pressure cooker, with panic and anxiety always simmering. I developed an unusual coping strategy: following a difficult altercation, I would quickly visit the washroom, have a quiet sob, apply some concealer and emerge ready for the next challenge. I needed to demonstrate resilience, a core company competence and as far as anyone could see, I was doing just that. No-one at work or at home knew just how bad I was feeling.

Then one day, in a meeting, the lid blew off the pressure cooker. Two co-workers were having a fairly heated conversation and I was simply listening in, observing the debate. All of a sudden, seemingly out of nowhere, I burst out crying and didn't stop for two hours. I eventually managed to leave the meeting and headed toward home – still crying. I made an appointment with my doctor before putting in a call to my two bosses. They were shocked and dumbfounded to hear I wasn't coping, they had no idea. I left the doctor's with some antidepressants and a referral for counselling and stopped off at a car park near home.

Before I could face my family, I needed to have one final cry.

A number of colourful expressions have been used to depict this state of mind: an overloaded machine that has finally blown; snapping under extreme pressure; an organ in convulsion; circuit overload; a feeling that the entire world is crashing down and you don't know how to save it.

Adjustment disorder doesn't do my experience any justice. It makes it sound as if I was getting stressed because my tie wasn't quite straight.

THE DARKNESS OF DEPRESSION

Taking three weeks off work to get myself back on the straight and narrow had failed miserably. The period of recuperation had no effect whatsoever on my mental wellbeing. My mind still felt broken. Mel and I returned to the doctor at a loss to understand what was happening. He recommended I take a break from work for a further unspecified period, prescribing a new combination of antidepressants and anti-anxiety pills. I had been diagnosed with agitated depression and, once again, I found myself on sick leave.

I made another difficult phone call to Andy, and once again he was very understanding. Despite being a start-up business, both partners agreed to take the financial hit and pay me a full salary while I was off work. God only knows what they must have been thinking. But although this was a huge relief, my overriding feeling had morphed into one of shock. This had all happened too quickly, and I was reeling.

Once things started to sink in, once the full enormity of recent events began to strike home, the relief of being signed off work was replaced by something far more sinister. Deep depression. Up until then, it had "only" been a case of extreme stress inflaming my anxiety, but now this was accompanied by a rapid downward spiralling of my mood. Winston Churchill called this his "black dog", a mental illness that loyally never leaves your side.

MENTAL HEALTH FACTS

There are many causes of depression, but, physiologically, it is mainly because of imbalances in certain brain chemicals called neurotransmitters:

- **Dopamine:** Helps regulate emotion, memory, thinking, motivation and reward.
- **Norepinephrine:** Makes your heart rate and blood pressure soar during a "fight or flight" response or stressful time.
- **Serotonin:** This "feel-good" chemical helps regulate your mood and plays a role in your overall sense of wellbeing.

Source: Verywell Mind

Just a few weeks previously, I had been a partner in a thriving fledgling consultancy, earning good money, with business on the up. And although it was proving to be a stressful experience, there was still everything to look forward to. Now, it looked like I was losing it all: my health, my career, my happiness, my self-esteem, my confidence. They were there one minute and gone the next, in the blink of an eye.

Several practical concerns piled on the pressure. Firstly, being the sole breadwinner, it was my responsibility to provide for the family. Even though I was being paid for the next few months, what would happen if I couldn't return to work once this period ended? How would we pay the mortgage? The bills? In my role as a husband and father, these were my responsibilities. Mel had others, all equally important. We had struck a deal and now

I wasn't keeping to my side of the bargain. It really felt as if I was letting everyone down.

The second concern was the thorny issue of medical insurance. I was not covered for mental illness to any significant degree by our insurers. If I needed to spend any time in a private hospital, we would have to fund this through our limited savings, and it could end up being a bottomless pit. In Worry's head, these concerns began to assume dramatic proportions, and scary monsters started popping up all over the place as I began to predict one nightmare scenario after another.

During those first few days and weeks, I became increasingly moronic, spending hours lying on my bed, staring at the ceiling, desperate for every day to end, and equally desperate for every new day not to begin. I felt trapped in mental and physical solitary confinement. On 22 May, six weeks into my sick leave, Andy called me suggesting we meet up to discuss how to take things forward. I felt terribly guilty that my continued absence was putting a huge burden on the business, and I am sure they wanted to resolve the situation as soon as possible. It was still very much in start-up mode, and this would have been the last thing my two partners needed. However, I was simply not in a fit state to go anywhere, speak to anybody or think about anything. I was very ill. It was agreed we would talk again in early July. Mel would keep in touch sporadically with Andy over the next few weeks, but there was never anything positive to report.

THE NEED FOR BLACK AND WHITE

I cannot stress enough how difficult those first couple of months were. I felt like a spider trapped in a bathtub, desperately trying to scale the sides as the water slowly rises but always slipping back down again.

During this desperate period, I visited an army of specialists, including a counsellor, a hypnotherapist, an expensive Harley Street psychiatrist and, at the suggestion of my mother-in-law, a retired faith healer. Remember this was before the days of Google when the only information resource was a huge directory called *Yellow Pages*. Just imagine me wading through the "counselling services" section (sandwiched in between "concrete suppliers" and "curtain fabrics"), frantically searching for somebody I could trust to end this painful experience.

The problem was that my personality required certainty and clarity of choice, but my depressed condition could only be managed through a process of trial and error. The illness was grey; I wanted black or white. I wanted exactitude; it could only offer approximation.

And each of the specialists had their own unique theory, their own plan for managing my illness and, not unreasonably, they wanted time to work with me on a long-term basis. Whenever I met somebody for the first time, I would spend the first half an hour or so providing background and context. It became a very well-rehearsed piece. I was impatient to get on with it and get better as quickly as possible, and if I didn't sense any immediate improvement, I would simply move on to the next expert. It became a bit like speed dating, albeit with quite a lot more at stake. And without the fun.

I would come to realize years later the importance of finding the right person to guide you through the illness. Not only did you want an expert with a CV packed full of stunning credentials and successes, but you also craved somebody who empathized and fully understood what you were going through. These people were very difficult to find.

"I didn't want to wake up. I was having a much better time asleep. And that's really sad. It was almost like a reverse nightmare, like when you wake up from a nightmare, you are so relieved. I woke up into a nightmare."

Ned Vizzini, writer

It would have been so much less stressful if I had broken my leg, however badly: a specialist would have sent me for an X-ray, before assessing the damage and deciding on the appropriate treatment, with check-ups every few weeks to review progress; a period of rehabilitation, and three to four months later my leg would have recovered. Life continues.

Mental illness is much more hit and miss. I just wanted to know that if I took medication A, B would happen, or if I undertook therapy X, then Y would happen. No such luck. It was more like playing a game of Snakes and Ladders, where moving up the board and tumbling down it were just down to a random throw of the dice.

Managing my agitated depression proved to be elusive. Days at home were long and laborious and I tried desperately hard to keep busy. I attempted to read the paper every morning, but my brain said no. I enrolled on a course to improve my PowerPoint skills in preparation for my return to work, but my brain said no again. Anything that required mental processing of any kind remained strictly out of bounds. Summer was approaching, and I would spend time in the garden, weeding, mowing the lawn, trimming the edges. I tried my best to engage in mindless activities designed to occupy, but not preoccupy, the brain.

It just about agreed to these.

During a period of just a few weeks, my brain had gone through a total metamorphosis. I remained downbeat every minute of every day, felt restless, agitated and perpetually tired. Empty and numb, I had lost all self-confidence and self-esteem and was a shell of my former self.

There was miniscule enjoyment in anything I did. I tried to keep fit; I went for a walk every day, crawling through the local countryside more slowly than a funeral march, always doing my best to avoid human contact; I went shopping with Mel to escape the monotony of doing nothing at home. I rarely engaged with my kids like any normal father might when they returned home from school. I was doing so little, but always felt so exhausted.

THE LANGUAGE OF IRRATIONAL

Another symptom of my mental illness was that I became increasingly introspective and self-focused. As I deteriorated, the only person I could talk to was Mel, and I became very demanding of her time. I would become irritated whenever the phone rang. The call was obviously never for me, and, more often than not, it was one of our friends enquiring how I was doing and making sure Mel was coping. As soon as she put the phone down, it was back to me. My time again. Jack, our two-year-old, and I would often compete for Mel's attention during the day. She was effectively in charge of four young children, and it was me, her "eldest child", who was causing her the most grief. I had gone from being a completely rational human being to one whose thoughts, feelings and behaviours were totally irrational. This was now the reality confronting Mel.

She remained inspirational throughout my illness. For what must have seemed like an eternity, she coped with the pressure the situation was placing on her, day in, day out. She looked after the kids, played with them, always trying to shield them from the difficulties at home. She managed the house, fed us all, drove us everywhere, kept me occupied, kept me safe. She became adept at reading the situation and playing what was in front of her. She was never sure what each day would bring, where my illness would take us next; as a result, she wasn't able to get into any routine. She planned where possible, but always reacted quickly whenever required. Mel put on a masterclass in multitasking under extreme duress.

And, importantly, she also slowly learned to speak my language of Irrational. Even though she initially struggled to understand why I couldn't just "pull myself together", she quickly learned that this "hard to fathom" illness was not a quick or easy fix. Talking, suggesting, advising and putting forward sensible solutions are all part of the language of Rational, but the depressed brain doesn't always respond well to logical argument. There is growing scientific evidence that several parts of the brain shrink in people with depression, and this can lead to a lack of clarity in thinking. In my experience, the more effective way of communicating with somebody who is experiencing depression is to listen without judgement, empathize, sympathize and just be there for them, without expecting anything in return. Repeating the words of Stephen Fry, you need to "understand the blackness, lethargy, hopelessness and loneliness they're going through".

You won't find the languages of Rational and Irrational listed in any literary work. They are two phrases I coined in 2019 on the back of my first book, *Breakdown and Repair*. However, I do believe that if society wants to improve the quality of the mental health conversation, then understanding how and when to speak Irrational, in particular, is a critical skill to develop. This is certainly the case for the more "logically minded" among us, who might find it difficult to sympathize and empathize with those who are experiencing the irrational thought patterns associated with mental illness.

A small band of close friends remained very supportive throughout this time, always checking in with Mel or scooping up the kids for a few hours while she accompanied me to yet another consultation. They would pop round for a coffee and chat, trying their hardest to engage me in conversation, doing their level best to normalize a situation that was abnormal. They didn't judge or become impatient, and were always there for Mel, me and the children. It must have been painfully difficult for them to see a friend now a pale shadow of his former self, and to witness the devastating effect this was having on his family. Everybody had to start learning my language of Irrational.

Pause for Thought

1. Do you think you might be experiencing depression or some other form of mental ill health right now?
2. If so, how are you feeling and what are some of the thoughts you have been having?
3. Have you sought help from a mental health or medical professional yet? Have you told any friends or family how you've been feeling? If not, consider doing so.

TRYING TOO HARD TO BOUNCE BACK

Once I had been on the new medication for about a month, I was strongly advised by my psychiatrist to enrol on a couple of courses at a hospital in Northampton, "Coping with Anxiety", and "Coping with Depression". The courses were based on an approach called Cognitive Behaviour Therapy (CBT).

CBT is a talking therapy that helps you better understand and manage your perceived problems by changing the way you think and behave. Numerous research studies suggest that CBT can lead to improved functioning and quality of life. It is based on the premise that your thoughts, feelings and physical actions are all interconnected. For example, if you think that you are not a popular person, then you may well shy away from social interaction, and this may lead to feelings of low-self-esteem. Or if you don't believe you are good at managing other people in the workplace, then you might be more inclined to avoid positions of responsibility, which, in the long run, might leave you feeling unfulfilled.

Through the process of CBT, you break down the negative patterns of thinking, feeling and doing, work out whether they

are unrealistic or unhelpful, and then put plans in place to make the necessary changes.

The group courses I attended in Northampton took place every week over a period of a couple of months, and in between the sessions there was "homework". One of the tasks was to complete a daily activity planner, scheduling in play, work and rest in blocks of 60 minutes. We were encouraged to be as disciplined as possible – completing the tasks was more important than enjoying them. The intention was that, each week, you would become more adventurous, your levels of enjoyment would slowly rise and, little by little, you would step back into normal life.

One of the psychiatrists I turned to during my illness had a colourful way of explaining the biology of restabilization. When deeply depressed, your brain is bombarded with black balls, miserable thoughts buzzing backwards and forwards. Over time, the combination of medication and therapies like CBT encourage an odd white ball of hope and happiness to appear.

Eventually, the white balls outnumber and overpower the black ones as the shoots of restabilization begin to take firm hold.

In theory, cognitive therapy made absolute sense, and later on in my life I became a fervent supporter of its rational approach. But right then, it just wasn't working for me. I did my best to fill in the daily schedule, stick to it and give the white balls every chance of overtaking black. However, sometimes even the most trivial of tasks were simply beyond me. All I really wanted to do was lie on my bed, close my eyes and go to sleep. Unfortunately, the illness only ever granted me four or five hours respite every night. *Everything* was such hard work, including sleeping.

And maybe that was why CBT didn't work for me. Its logical approach was probably too taxing, requiring too much thinking. I simply wasn't up for it and needed a complete break from anything that was remotely challenging. Once again, my brain said no.

The two courses came to an end, and by this point I should have been edging back toward what I considered to be normality. But I wasn't. My doctors were now scratching their collective heads, unsure which new medication to prescribe, which talking therapy to recommend next. The white balls were nowhere in sight. The colour was still black.

Pause for Thought

1. Are you currently receiving help for your depression or mental health condition? If so, what kind?
2. Which courses or therapies have been recommended to you?
3. If you're not receiving help, why is that? What is stopping you from trying any of these recommendations?

I can only imagine how difficult it must have been for both my business partners during this period when they would have had so much else to deal with. The cost of my absence would have caused them a real headache. The worry and uncertainty that comes with any mental illness make it very tricky to deal with, to predict. I felt very guilty that I was letting them both down badly. Guilt is often depression's partner in crime.

A few weeks into my sick leave, Andy and Mhairi needed to become more procedural in their communication and correspondence with me in order to protect the interests of the business. It was now mid-June. I had been on sick leave for just over two months when I received a letter from my two partners. A 12-week sick leave period had previously been agreed and now there was the option of a further four weeks, taking this up to 30 July, if required.

Again, this was a relief to Mel and me from a financial point of view. Although the tone of the letter was very supportive, it was made clear that the current situation was creating financial and managerial pressures for the company and that it was in everyone's best interest to resolve what my future role would be, both "swiftly and amicably". It was suggested a meeting should be planned for early July to explore some options and decide on a way forward.

The clock was now ticking, but unfortunately, the last thing a stressed brain needs is a ticking clock.

HELP YOURSELF

TRY THE DEPRESSION SYMPTOM CHECKER

Depression can creep up on you beneath the radar. If you are worried that you might be on the verge of becoming depressed, why not use the table below. The contents are sourced from advice provided on three separate websites:

The British National Health Service, Mind, the UK's leading mental health charity and WebMD, an American organization dedicated to the provision of health advice online. The crosses in the table applied to me at the beginning of my depressive episode.

DEPRESSION SYMPTOM CHECKER	
THOUGHTS (mental)	**FEELINGS (physical)**
• Trouble concentrating **X**	• Fatigue and tiredness **X**
• Trouble remembering	• Lack of energy **X**
• Being indecisive **X**	• Aches, pains, cramps
• Suicidal thinking **X**	• Digestive problems
ACTIONS/INACTION (observable)	**FEELINGS (emotional)**
• Sleeping badly **X**	• Guilt **X**
• Eating too much/little **X**	• Worthlessness **X**
• No enjoyment in doing things **X**	• Helplessness and hopelessness **X**
• Loss of libido **X**	• Emptiness **X**
• Avoiding social contact **X**	• Restlessness
• Smoking more, drinking more alcohol	• Crankiness
• Tearfulness	• Anxiety **X**
• Self-harming	• Sadness **X**

WHAT TO DO

1. Read every item in each of the four quadrants and put an "X" next to any that describe your current thoughts, feelings or behaviours.
2. Share the completed list with a close friend or family member and ask them to corroborate what you have written.

3. With the help of this person, decide quickly whether you may be in need of professional help. Seek help immediately if you are either self-harming or having suicidal thoughts. Call the Samaritans on 116 123 in the UK or 1 (800) 273-TALK in the USA.

A COUPLE OF WATCHOUTS

A. This checklist should not be a replacement for professional help; treat it more as part of your early warning system.
B. If necessary, ask a couple of people to provide their perspective. Honest and objective feedback from others can be invaluable.

KEY TAKEAWAYS

1. **A nervous breakdown feels very real**: It also serves a purpose because your brain is telling you that enough is enough, and it will only reboot once you're out of danger.

2. **The language of mental ill health can be an irrational one:** Friends, co-workers and family members more fluent in the language of Rational must also learn the language of Irrational if they're going to communicate more empathetically with a person experiencing a depressive episode.

3. **Pick the right resources to help you manage your illness:** Finding the right medical professional(s) to guide you through your illness is critical, and picking therapies that work for you, equally so.

5

DEEP DEPRESSION AND BIG DECISIONS

Get support when making decisions during a depressive episode

Depression can take you down into the darkest of tunnels, where the only shade of colour is the blackest of blacks. This chapter will demonstrate why, when combined with drugs and big decision-making, depression can become a dodgy and dangerous mix. That was certainly the case for me.

1. **Employment:** I had to make major decisions about my job when I was experiencing a severe depressive episode.
2. **Medical support:** Significant choices about medication and care were made when I wasn't always capable of making them for myself.
3. **Life or death:** I was making these decisions at a time when I was also considering trying to end my life.

The clinical argument for not making important decisions when you are experiencing a depressive disorder is compelling. The hippocampus, located near the centre of the brain, is responsible for cognitive functions such as learning, memory and the regulation of behaviour. It's been found that chronic stress can cause long-term damage to the hippocampus, and has been known to reduce its overall size.

> *"Depression is such a cruel punishment. There are no fevers, no rashes, no blood tests to send people scurrying in concern, just the slow erosion of self, as insidious as cancer. And like cancer, it is essentially a solitary experience, a room in hell with only your name on the door."*
>
> Martha Manning, psychologist and writer

The prefrontal cortex makes up over 10% of the volume of the brain and is responsible for controlling executive functions like planning, decision-making and problem-solving. Stress has a negative shrinking effect on the prefrontal cortex. And the amygdala, the part of the brain that facilitates emotional responses – like pleasure and fear – and the detection of threat, actually increases in size, making the brain even more receptive to stress.

But depression is much more than just a brain disorder. It affects your physical wellbeing too, and can lead to an increased risk of heart disease, high blood pressure and diabetes, as well as impairing the body's immune system. In short, chronic stress really isn't good news either for the brain or for the body.

BIG DECISION NUMBER 1: RETURN TO WORK OR RESIGN

It was the end of June and I had been off work for over two and a half months. There were now just three weeks to go until I was due to meet up with my partners to decide on next steps as far as the job was concerned. The clock was ticking louder and louder in my confused and crowded brain as D-day approached. Depression doesn't do deadlines very well.

A violent struggle was raging in my head between two powerful opponents, each desperate to knock the other one out. One side was called "Must Go Back", the other, "Can't Go Back". They fought furiously, non-stop, for three weeks, neither prepared to give an inch of ground. "Can't Go Back" was up on points, but "Must Go Back" was putting up one hell of a fight. He was on the ropes but wasn't giving up. Not just yet.

As a result, I quickly deteriorated, and in moments of extreme stress the headbanging returned with a vengeance. I would simply find the nearest wall and hit my head against it repeatedly. I am not sure what the psychological explanation for this was. Maybe it was just a physical manifestation of my mental distress, or another frantic attempt to try to bring the nightmare to an end. Whatever it was, it was weird, and it freaked Mel out – she tried her best to hide my bizarre behaviour from the children.

The consultant psychiatrist at Isham House in Northampton, who had supervised me while I was undertaking the CBT classes, saw me at the beginning of July. This was what he wrote in his clinical report.

"He has fitful and unrefreshing sleep with quite frequent early morning waking, his mood is low, but is at its worst in the morning. He eats with no relish at all, has seriously impaired concentration with both distractibility and sluggish thinking, no real interest in anything, very little energy, and feelings of hopelessness associated with frequent suicidal thinking, but no active planning." The correct clinical term for this behaviour is "passive suicidal ideation", when a person talks about taking their own life but has made no concrete plans to do so.

Fast forward to 9 July, the date of my planned meeting with Andy and Mhairi was edging closer and closer. I had made no progress. In fact, I had gone backwards and was in no fit mental state to have any kind of coherent conversation with anyone about anything of consequence.

So Mel telephoned Andy in a state of desperation and told him I wouldn't be able to meet with him and Mhairi as planned. Andy offered his support to Mel, but mentioned that my absence was having a considerable impact on the business. He asked Mel if she could find the right moment to talk to me and find out how I wanted to proceed. He then went on to outline a number of broad options to facilitate my return to the business. Either I could resume my role as a full director or return as a director with reduced responsibilities/equity. Alternatively, I could resign as a director and come back as an employee in some kind of flexible capacity once I had recovered. If I were to go for the last of these options, I would need to sell my equity back to Andy and Mhairi as per our Shareholders' Agreement.

At this time, I was barely capable of making my own breakfast, let alone making decisions that would determine my career and the rest of our lives. I was feeling under enormous pressure to come to a decision, and quickly too.

SIMON'S STORY

The danger of returning to work too soon

I went back to work on a Monday after two weeks off; just two weeks after I had filled the Thames with my tears, after standing up at my desk and announcing to the rest of the office that "I can't deal with this shit, someone else is going to have to step in." As promised, my introduction back into the office was all very relaxed without even a passing mention of why I had been off. That soon changed as my anxiety built. By Thursday I was beginning to feel like I needed to pull my weight and couldn't afford to appear like a passenger. I had to demonstrate that I was getting better and that I was well enough to be adding value.

The first client brief was straightforward. Work I had done a hundred times before. But here's the thing. It had to be done by the middle of next week. The anxiety descended immediately, I started sweating and my attention switched to making sure others didn't see that, rather than the job in hand. Despite my best efforts to deliver the work, I imploded. Here's a few of my thoughts at the time:

"If I don't deliver this, what will people think of me?"

"There is too much at stake for them to have to carry me on the team."

"What's wrong with me? My co-workers could knock this out in two hours."

Although the work was finally delivered and the client was happy, I was once again broken. What followed was a further six months off, much of it spent in a much darker place.

I hadn't been able to contemplate anything business-related for over three months, and the thought of even discussing work filled me with horror. I was convinced the man-eating lion was still lurking in my home office, ferociously guarding my computer. I didn't dare check. My fast-deteriorating brain was far too ill to consider the options my two partners were putting on the table, or at least understand their implications.

However, during the next 24 hours, Mel and I somehow managed to talk things through. We weighed up the options as best we could, and in a misguided attempt to alleviate my stress, and in the desperate hope this might help my recovery, we finally made a very difficult decision.

I called Andy the following day with conflicting emotions flooding through my head. I told him I wasn't able to give him any indication of when I would be able to return to work and in what capacity. I felt that to be fair to my partners, the only option I had was to resign over the phone.

During the same conversation, we agreed we needed to reach closure on the uncertainty surrounding the business. We agreed I would be unable to operate as a director. We agreed that the necessary steps would be taken to value my equity and review the implications on the business. We agreed I would take the appropriate legal and professional advice. We agreed rather a lot on that phone call, even though my mind was totally scrambled.

That July, mirtazapine was treating my depression, buspirone my anxiety, and zopiclone would help me get a maximum of four hours' sleep a night. Following further diagnosis, olanzapine, the antipsychotic drug, was introduced to address my increasingly frenzied behaviour – more headbanging, relentless pacing up and down, staring into space. Lithium carbonate, a mood stabilizer, was waiting in the wings just in case I turned out to be bipolar too; I wasn't.

So at the point I was making critical decisions around both employment and shareholding, my hippocampus and prefrontal cortex had both shrunk, leading to memory loss and poor decision-making; the inflated size of my amygdala meant I was completely exhausted; and all parts of my brain were being bombarded by a powerful cocktail of drugs. Whichever way you look at things, it wasn't a great time for me to be discussing commercially complex matters or taking key decisions that would affect the next chapter of my life.

A few weeks later, I received a letter from the company confirming everything we had discussed over the phone.

Although "Must Go Back" had finally conceded, "Can't Go Back" had won what almost turned out to be a Pyrrhic victory. Worry had triumphed over Winner, but our decision to make a decision about the job had been the wrong one. It had harmed rather than helped, confused rather than clarified. I now felt under more rather than less pressure.

The gamble that Mel and I had taken hadn't paid off and a dramatic sequence of events would now unfold.

Pause for Thought

1. If you are experiencing any mental illness, is your employer or line manager aware of your situation?
2. At this time, are you experiencing any pressure from your line manager or employer, either to leave the company, stay or change your role within it?
3. What have these conversations looked like? Why are they occurring? Do you feel able to advocate for yourself in these conversations? If not, have you enlisted the support of the correct medical, mental health and legal professionals to assist you in the process?

BIG DECISION NUMBER 2: ADMIT OR DON'T ADMIT TO HOSPITAL

Called "the perfect place to die", Aokigahara, a forest also referred to as the Sea of Trees, sits right along the edge of Mount Fuji, two hours west of Tokyo. Throughout the forest, signs have been mounted on the trees: "Life is a precious gift", "Quietly think once more about your parents, siblings or children", "Please consult the police before you decide to die". Since the turn of the century, up to 105 bodies have been found in the forest every year.

Experts have long considered why some choose to come to this vast forest to end their life. Three decades ago, a Japanese psychiatrist who interviewed a handful of Aokigahara suicide survivors concluded that "they believed that they would be able to die successfully without being noticed".

It was 16 July, 16 months after the Runnymede meeting when Andy, Mhairi and I had begun our great adventure.

I was now back in the care of the Tindal Centre, the Mental Health Unit for adults in Aylesbury. I was examined by the Locum Staff Grade Psychiatrist. It was a one-off emergency appointment. This is an extract of his letter sent to my GP:

"Over the weekend, things appear to have erupted when Mr Simmonds became extremely agitated, hyperventilating and his behaviour became markedly frenzied. He started shouting at the children, stating that he believed he was the devil and that his nervous system didn't work anymore. He tried to test this by stabbing himself with a knife or attempting to cut himself on the arms ... He appeared to be fairly agitated and showed markedly impaired concentration with disjointed thinking and was continuously preoccupied."

Another member of the psychiatric team described my deteriorating condition as "worsening depersonalization verging on nihilism". He made it sound like I was having some kind of existentialist experience. In layman's terms, life had become meaningless.

I had been on sick leave for three and a half months. My home had become a prison and I was in solitary confinement. One week earlier, in a state of utter desperation, I had felt compelled to resign from Brand Learning. The future was looking bleak, making the present feel unbearable.

At the meeting with the psychiatrist, he recommended I admit myself to the Tindal Centre for an inpatient stay. I was becoming a real danger to myself, Mel and the kids. Mel confessed she was frightened having me at home. She felt unsafe and was unsure how much longer she could cope with the situation. She was already hiding knives and anything else sharp in the home to protect both me and the family. She had been on a 24-hour vigil for weeks and was now exhausted.

The Tindal Centre (now closed) was inhabited by patients with extreme psychological disorders and it played an extremely valuable role in the community. There weren't any other similar facilities available in the vicinity. Unfortunately, I was a middle-class Englishman enjoying a middle-class kind of life, and the thought of being admitted into an inpatient mental health unit terrified me. Mel and I went away to consider our options. In a strangely calm manner, we drove to a small café in a neighbouring village to have a cup of coffee and consider the advantages and disadvantages of admission. We looked like a "normal" couple having an everyday conversation, and anybody listening in might have gasped if they had heard what we were discussing.

Although I was extremely depressed, there were still times when I could be totally lucid. These would contrast starkly with other times when the unrelenting pressure of the situation led to unpredictable, erratic and peculiar behaviours – headbanging, self-stabbing, grunting.

After a lengthy debate, we decided against admission, but mainly for the wrong reasons. The stigma associated with places like the Tindal Centre was very strong at the time. A long stay there was not going to sit very comfortably on my CV, and this was a frightening prospect now that my career was in tatters.

With the benefit of hindsight, we made a very poor decision that day, but ended up being extraordinarily lucky.

I now resembled a total zombie, communicating with nobody, simply going through the motions. I felt marooned, my isolation from society complete, both physically and mentally. My business co-workers were the first to be left behind, closely followed by my friends, and then my three kids. Now it was Mel's turn.

I had been sleeping alone at night for several months, and every evening I would go to bed at midnight, dosed up with zopiclone. This remained effective until 4am when I would wake up, unable to sleep any longer, my mind back at Le Mans. I would get out of bed and pace the room. Up and down, up and down. Ruminating, worrying, catastrophizing. Mel would sleep in another room, door ajar, in case I decided to tiptoe downstairs looking for knives. Physically, we were apart, and now I let Mel slip out of my life emotionally too.

The summer holidays had just started, and the children were going to be at home for the next six weeks. Their proximity to me was adding to my feelings of self-loathing, and my proximity to them – as well as my strange antics – were only adding to their sense of confusion. This wasn't how fathers were supposed to behave. I felt utterly useless and, due to my distorted way of thinking, as though I had failed my family miserably. My guilt was unbearable. There was nowhere left to hide.

Pause for Thought

1. Are you having any form of suicidal thoughts?
2. Have you told anyone how you are feeling?

Help is immediately available. Call someone now. Try the Samaritans on 116 123 in the UK or 1 (800) 273-TALK in the USA.

BIG DECISION NUMBER 3: LIVE OR DIE

On 19 July, around 10am, I found myself home alone when Mel took the kids to a friend's to escape the madhouse for a few hours. Later, Mel would openly share the guilt she felt about leaving me on my own that day.

I was feeling suicidal. The walls had all closed in. There was now no way out. This all had to end. Passive suicide activation had moved to active suicide ideation. I was now ready to hatch a plan and carry it out.

> "There comes a point when you no longer care if there's a light at the end of the tunnel or not. You are just sick of the tunnel."
>
> Ranata Suzuki, poet

We had an Oxford Hammond *Atlas of The World* sitting on one of our bookshelves in the living room. I thumbed my way through it until I found the most detailed map of the UK. I was looking for Beachy Head, a popular suicide spot on the south coast. I thought through the logistics carefully, but realized it was too far away and too complicated to get there. I ditched that idea pretty quickly.

Time for Plan B. Something closer to home. I decided to cycle toward the nearest railway line, just outside Soulbury, a neighbouring village, 20 minutes away. The InterCity trains would pelt down this section of the track, travelling in excess of 100mph south to London or north to Manchester and beyond.

The end would be mercifully quick at least.

However, once I had reached my destination, I realized there was no easy access down to the tracks. It was then that I noticed a parked police car with a couple of officers inside. They appeared to be observing me, knowing I was up to some kind of mischief. Could this have been the illness talking? Was I simply hallucinating, becoming paranoid? Whatever it was, I hesitated. I gave up on Plan B. Time for another rethink.

I turned around and started making my way back home, feeling frustrated. I still hadn't found my Aokigahara. Ending my life wasn't proving to be the straightforward task I had imagined.

Fortunately, I had a Plan C. One last plan before I would have to concede defeat, return home, face the kids and Mel, and endure more pain and misery in what had become my prison. I decided to cycle the long way home, winding my way through the local villages. On this route, there was a stretch of road I had driven many times. A long and straight B-road where cars and lorries always drove too fast. Final chance.

It was exhausting stuff. Most of the ride was uphill and I was very unfit, full up to the brim with medication, my mind contaminated with dark thoughts. My poor brain was going haywire. But there wasn't a wretched speeding lorry in sight. Where the hell were they when you needed them most?

Eventually, I crawled my way into the village of Wing which somewhat ironically was where the doctor's surgery was located.

Then, at last, the moment I had been waiting for … There it was … Rumbling toward me … Here we go …

The next thing I knew, I was in the John Radcliffe specialist trauma unit in Oxford, having been involved in a collision with a 10-ton truck. I had suffered head injuries and a tension pneumothorax (collapsed lung) and had been transported to the hospital by air ambulance. It had been a first-class accident, but suicide was obviously not meant for me.

When Mel and the kids returned home, they found a police car sitting on the drive. The policemen informed Mel that I had been involved in a major incident, but that I was alive and in intensive care with serious injuries. Somewhat ironically, the psychiatric nurse supervising me at the time was also waiting outside the house. We had an appointment to check on how I was doing. Not very well, by all accounts.

Our decision not to admit me into the care of the Tindal Centre had been a mistake. At least I would have been safe there, depriving me of the opportunity to do anything reckless. That reason should have trumped everything, including the "shame" and stigma of spending time inside a mental institution.

Let's talk about suicide. The myth is that people who attempt it are cowards without any thought for the people they are leaving behind. That they have no understanding of the impact their actions will have on their nearest and dearest, who are left with feelings of guilt for the rest of their lives.

Incorrect. Here is the truth: the vast majority of people who try to take their own life are mentally very unwell. The chemical imbalance affecting your brain makes it impossible for you to think rationally because your mind is not functioning properly. The neurotransmitters aren't doing their job. When you break your leg, you can't walk; when you are horribly depressed, you can't think.

In fact, it's worse than that – you can think, but you can't think straight. Your thinking is completely distorted. The extreme depression is lying to you, convincing you that you're a burden on all those around you, that you're dragging them down, that the world would be an infinitely better place without you.

> "Depression lies. It's a horrible asshole bitch that breaks people – it breaks good people, strong people, loving people. It does not discriminate. It's an equal opportunity fucker."
>
> Christine Skoutelas, blogger and freelance writer

By the time you attempt to take your own life, you have already departed from this world. You have done so because you believe you're doing the right thing, the selfless thing. Your impaired mind is telling you this every minute of every day. Eventually, you believe it because it becomes too painful not to.

But if you *are* thinking about it, don't do it. Don't throw yourself in front of a truck, don't jump off a tall building, don't take an overdose. Even though you might have found yourself trapped in the darkest of caves, there will be a ladder somewhere to the surface. That ladder might be a combination of time, talking therapies, medication and the love of those around you, but it will be there. And when you get to the top, you might just be surprised by what you find up there. I certainly was.

Final point. I would like to apologize to the lorry driver for the distress this incident must have caused you. I hope this narrative makes it crystal clear that it was not your fault.

MENTAL HEALTH FACTS

- In 2019, the age-standardized suicide rate, globally, was 2.3 times higher in males than it was in females.
- The male suicide rate in 2019 of 16.9 deaths per 100,000 in England and Wales was the highest since 2000.
- Men aged 45–49 remain at the highest risk of suicide, but there has been an increase in suicide rates among young people, especially women aged under 25.

Source: Office for National Statistics Report (2020), World Health Organization

BIG DECISION NUMBER 4: DECIDING NOT TO DECIDE

The Trauma Service Unit at the John Radcliffe Hospital in Oxford provides treatment for patients who have sustained life-threatening physical injuries. A 24-hour service is provided by a dedicated team of consultants and specialists, including both neurosurgeons and plastic surgeons for reconstructive surgery after serious injuries. I needed the former, but fortunately not the latter. I would remain there for two weeks.

The first thing I remember when I regained consciousness was talking to Mel and one of her closest friends who had accompanied her to the hospital. The second thing I remember was making a rather lewd joke and all of us laughing out aloud. The third thing I recall was getting mildly frustrated with the head nurse who I felt was not being sympathetic enough.

Conversing, laughing, complaining. On the face of it, nothing special, nothing worth writing home about. But they represented three small signs of life, three "normal" behaviours I had not displayed in months. Not only was I utterly relieved to be physically alive, a miracle in itself, but more importantly, I was thrilled to be alive emotionally again. I was now emerging into the sunlight.

My injuries, although not life-threatening, were still serious. I remained bed-bound during my first week in hospital. My lung was being drained, my head wounds were healing slowly, and I was still in a lot of pain. From time to time, I would burst out crying for no particular reason. I was very fragile and had a whole bunch of horrible memories festering away in the back of my head. Initially, the doctors took me off all the medication I had been on before the accident. Mel intuitively sensed something about me was different and she encouraged them not to put me back on the cocktail of drugs, but to see how things progressed. They listened to her and agreed with her non-expert diagnosis.

But it was the second week of my stay I remember with greatest clarity, because it signalled a gradual return to the wonderful bliss of the everyday mundane. Once again, I was beginning to appreciate the little things in life.

What did this look like? I was able to walk, so would pass the time of day cruising the sterile hospital corridors, attached to my drip, smiling inanely and chatting happily with the other patients and nurses about nothing in particular. I would buy the newspaper and turn straight to the sports pages, just like the good old days. I would treat myself to a Mars bar at 11am every morning in the hospital cafeteria, go for a gentle stroll in the hospital garden every afternoon, soak in the sunshine, smell the flowers, and suck in the fresh air. I would get visits from my family and friends at teatime and talk about the day's news and the weather. I would sleep soundly for ten hours without the fear of waking up.

I now had a "proper" physical illness. It was much simpler to explain away a bicycle accident and a collapsed lung to fellow patients than it was to talk about the impact of stress at work and the symptoms of agitated depression. And colliding head-on with a truck made for colourful corridor conversations, but obviously I decided to miss out the suicide bit. I think I was still in denial. In years to come, it would be much easier to talk about mental illness without embarrassment, but society wasn't quite ready for that kind of conversation back then.

No doubt about it, my two-week stay in hospital marked a turning point. Being knocked off my bike was the pivotal moment. I will never really understand what flicked the switch back on. Was it the physical impact caused by the accident to my brain? Some kind of high-risk shock therapy?

Was it the awful realization that I had come within a whisker of losing my life, my wife and my kids that had finally brought me to my senses? Or was it something else? Something more divine?

It was now the beginning of August, time to recuperate and start the slow process of getting back to a healthy state, mentally and physically. Having spent a fortnight in hospital, I was given permission to return home. Mel would spend a further two weeks driving me to Oxford on a daily two-hour round trip to receive intravenous drip antibiotics. These were treating a bacterial infection called empyema I had picked up in hospital.

My two business partners had kept in touch with Mel during this period, and Andy had paid me a visit when I was still in hospital. They had both been understandably shocked to hear about my accident, and were oblivious to the fact that it had been a suicide attempt. It was not something I owned up to at that time. In fact, this little secret of mine would remain hidden for many years to come. In hindsight, I wish I had shared this earlier than I eventually did. It would probably have completed my catharsis, and possibly helped others too.

Meanwhile, a detailed letter outlining the process for my departure from Brand Learning and the purchase of my shareholding had arrived in the post. This confirmed the details of my telephone conversation with Andy a few weeks earlier when I was so desperately ill. Neither Mel nor I were ready yet to deal with such matters. In just under four months, I had not opened my computer once or looked at anything vaguely work-related. My body and mind were still healing. So, this letter was put to one side for the time being. At last, we had got one big decision right. The decision not to decide. Not yet anyway.

It remains a mystery why this period didn't signal a return to the living nightmare. After all, nothing was significantly different. My situation at home had not changed. I had simply been given a brief respite, a fortnight off from the solitude and desperation. I had no job to go back to and no financial security blanket ahead.

Pause for Thought

1. Do you have any big decisions pending at the moment?
2. Are you in the right frame of mind to make them?
3. Have you received the necessary professional advice to help you make the correct decision?

But life *wasn't* the same anymore. Those feelings of utter misery had now left me, and I felt purged. Admittedly, I experienced a few wobbles after my departure from hospital, some tears and a sudden panic attack or two. The memories of the last few months and the surreal drama of the previous few weeks were still very raw, and we also remained concerned about what the future might have in store. Nevertheless, things had slowly started to feel different. The fog had lifted slightly. I was beginning to think and act like a normal human being again – or like a newly born foal taking its first tentative steps into a strange, new world, not completely steady on its feet, but getting there, bit by bit.

After finally being signed off by the hospital, the family decided to go to Bournemouth on the south coast for a few days. I was now able to join my kids making sandcastles on the beach, enjoy a Cornetto ice cream or two, feel the warm sun on my face and take a mid-afternoon nap when needed.

Precious little luxuries. My mind was now totally devoid of any big, bad and ugly thoughts, and in their place was a glorious feeling of nothing very important. The hippocampus, prefrontal cortex and amygdala were finally at peace with one another.

The war was over.

HELP YOURSELF

TRY A DECISION LADDER
The Decision Ladders below refer to two decisions we got wrong. I outline:
a) The questions we should have asked.
b) The honest answers we would have given at the time.
c) The decisions we should have taken, but didn't.

Decision Ladder

Should I decide to resign or not, while unwell?

1. Are you mentally fit enough to make a big decision by yourself?
Not at all.

2. Do you have to make the decision now? Can it wait?
From my point of view, it could wait. From my business partners' perspective, they want me to decide because of the pressure the company is being put under.

3. Are you being advised by a member of your family?
Yes, my wife is doing her best in very difficult circumstances.

4. Are you taking independent professional advice?
No, we aren't taking advice on all the important issues.

5. Will the decision affect your health positively or negatively?
We think that, strangely enough, it might serve to take the pressure off.

What decision should you have taken?
I should have agreed to stop receiving sick pay, but should have made no further decisions until I'd recovered.

Decision Ladder

Should I admit myself into the psychiatric hospital?

1. Are you mentally fit enough to make a big decision by yourself?
Not at all.

2. Do you have to make the decision now? Can it wait?
No, it can't wait because things are becoming critical and I am becoming a danger to myself and those around me.

3. Are you being advised by a member of your family?
Yes, my wife, but she feels very torn and uncertain about what to do.

4. Are you taking independent professional advice?
Yes, the doctors and specialists have the strong view that I should admit myself.

5. Will the decision affect your health positively or negatively?
We think that admission would have a negative rather than positive effect, without realizing that at least I would be safe in the hospital.

What decision should you have taken?
I should have admitted myself as soon as the opportunity was offered.

WHAT TO DO

1. Identify any significant decisions that you feel under pressure to take. These could be medical, legal, financial or linked to your job.
2. Working with a family member, co-worker or close friend, take your time to answer each of the five questions in the Decision Ladder.
3. Use this information to help you "make a decision about the decision".

A COUPLE OF WATCHOUTS

A. Your number one priority is always to protect your mental wellbeing; don't jeopardize this at any time.
B. Take your time to gather all the information you require before you make any decisions. Don't be rushed, particularly if you are mentally unwell.

KEY TAKEAWAYS

- **If in doubt, don't decide:** The brain is a super-complex organ, and when "under attack" its performance becomes erratic. Any big life or business decision that can be put off should be put off.
- **Surround yourself by people who can help you make healthy decisions:** If you are mentally very unwell, trust the experts to help you make the right medical choices if you feel currently incapable of doing so yourself.
- **Understand the psychology of suicide:** Somebody who is suicidal is not thinking clearly or rationally. It is not a selfish act. Their depressed mind is feeding them destructive lies which feel very believable.

RESURFACING INTO THE WORKPLACE

Obtain the right professional guidance after a period of mental illness

The period of recuperation immediately after a major depressive episode and subsequent re-entry back into the workplace is a critical time when it's important to receive the right guidance from the right people. As far as I was concerned, it was also important that Winner and Worry were given sound

advice. They had both received a battering during the Big Blip.

This chapter will cover the following areas:

1. **Mental health management:** Making sure you get the right support, either with medication or appropriate therapy, or both.
2. **The need for legal and financial expertise:** If any legal or financial matters need sorting out, ensuring that independent professionals are there to guide you.

3. **Restarting the "mental engine":** Working together with your employers to help you manage re-entry to the workplace safely with your best interests at heart.

4. **Career counselling:** View this time as an opportunity to reassess and re-evaluate your career by taking guidance from people far enough removed to see the wood from the trees, but close enough to steer you in the right direction.

Let's first talk about deep-sea diving.

Decompression sickness (DCS), more commonly known as the bends, is a type of injury that occurs when there is a rapid decrease in pressure surrounding the body. Gas bubbles can begin to form in the blood and tissues, leading to pain in the muscles and joints, problems with vision and extreme fatigue. This usually occurs in deep-sea divers who ascend to the surface too quickly, hikers coming down from high altitude or space astronauts returning to Earth.

> *"You don't have to see the whole staircase,*
> *just take the first step."*
>
> Martin Luther King Jr, Baptist minister and activist

To prevent DCS, it is recommended to take a number of decompression stops before ascending to the surface. If you have been diving deep, this needs to happen a few times to ensure that your body has time to adjust bit by bit. The last decompression stop is usually about 15 feet (4.5m) below the surface.

Best practice for a person re-entering the workplace after a period of mental ill health should follow exactly the same procedure. You must reacclimatize to the pressures of work slowly and steadily, carefully nurtured and supported by those around you. When somebody has experienced a full-blown mental breakdown, "returning to the surface" too quickly is particularly dangerous if the environment at the surface was the primary cause of the breakdown.

MENTAL HEALTH MANAGEMENT

The honeymoon – that special holiday when everything is perfect. You've just enjoyed the best day of your life, marrying the one you love, surrounded by family and close friends. You get some ringfenced time to reminisce about the great day itself, indulge yourself wherever you happen to be, and look forward to what lies ahead.

Everything new goes through a honeymoon phase of sorts, whether it's the joyful arrival of a new baby, the first few weeks in a job, or the thrill of picking up a brand-new car. My convalescence during the first three weeks of August was my equivalent, and the feeling was no less exciting. In my case, what was new was life itself. I now preferred waking up to being asleep. And I was back to experiencing and enjoying all the little things in life, like going to the pub, mowing the lawn, taking a stroll in the countryside. I felt all the excitement and trepidation of a kid riding a bike for the first time.

If the "honeymoon" proved to be the first important step in helping me stabilize, medication was the second. Throughout the latter stages of my illness, I was drowning in a cocktail of different drugs in a desperate but ultimately futile attempt to treat either my anxiety, depression, insomnia or paranoia. Immediately after the accident, I was taken off all medication and my system was given the chance to cleanse itself of all the chemicals. The doctors decided to introduce me to a new drug, the slow-release version of Efexor XL, which I was to take for the next six months. This was intended to keep my mood steady and stable and was taken mainly for preventative purposes.

There is still widespread debate over the use of medication to treat mental ill health, and even though pills and tablets seemed to have little positive impact on me when my depression was at its most acute, I have always put my trust in the doctors and the science. In the future, I would never have any hesitation in resorting to medication if I felt it could stabilize things. In my view, if the brain's neurotransmitters needed a dose of something to get them back on their feet, the sooner the better.

During this period, I remained assigned to my psychiatric nurse, Robin Lim, and his job was to keep a watchful eye on me, making sure I didn't inspect any more railway lines too closely. We would meet every couple of weeks to review progress and check how I was doing. This relationship lasted until I was well clear of the danger zone. My brain was still healing, and this would take time.

Another important element in my "restoration" was my attitude toward the breakdown. Mental illness was a pretty taboo subject at that time, but I decided to be very open about what had happened to me. I didn't really have much choice as it had been a very public affair. I had helped start a fledgling business with two high-profile partners, which was going extremely well, and then had bailed out early, taking four months' sick leave before having a major road accident. If I had then returned to the world of employment as a freelancer, claiming that "I had a bad virus that took a frustratingly long time to clear up", it would not have fooled anyone.

The second reason I opened up was because I didn't think I had anything to be ashamed of. I felt strongly that everyone, including me, had more to gain if I was completely transparent and honest. I remember one episode where I spilled the beans about my story to a small group of young graduates at the end of a day's training. Rather than being uncomfortable with what I was sharing, they remained captivated and curious when I explained what had happened and the lessons I had learned. I included most of the dark bits, but missed out the attempted suicide. At the time, I was still processing this and it certainly didn't feel appropriate to discuss it with others.

And the third reason I was comfortable talking about my Big Blip was because it felt wonderfully cathartic, providing a cleansing of any destructive emotions that were still lurking in the undergrowth. This catharsis was often accompanied by a tear or two because things were still very raw. But, as they say, it's always better out than in.

MENTAL HEALTH FACTS

- 51% of managers have had a mental health problem like stress, anxiety or depression disclosed to them by co-workers.
- 62% of managers who have had a member of staff disclose a mental health problem to them have either never received any training, or received it over 12 months prior.
- 52% of male managers have never received mental health training, compared to 42% of female managers.

Source: Chartered Management Institute (CMI)

A REIGNITED RELATIONSHIP

During the period of my illness, Mel had been the rock that held everything together – the family, the house and, as far as it was possible, me. Somehow, she also managed to find the energy to hold herself together throughout the crisis.

She now experienced conflicting emotions. On the one hand, there was the unbridled joy and relief that she had got her husband back in one piece. She had been just a tyre's width away from becoming a widow and facing the prospect of having to bring up three young children on her own. She too now relished the simple, uncomplicated things in life again, a return to some kind of "normal" existence. No more hiding knives, or talking to psychiatrists about self-harming, or visiting suicidal husbands in trauma units. On the other hand, she still endured feelings of uncertainty. Was my upbeat mood going to last, or would it be a false dawn? Was something ugly hiding round the next corner? For her, the enormous contrast between life before and after the accident was hard to fathom.

I felt exactly the same. Sometimes, I needed to pinch myself just to make sure that this wasn't some kind of cruel dream out of which I would shortly awake and return to the living nightmare. It was too good to be true.

However, there was one marital silver lining that emerged from the fallout which helped keep us both grounded. We started talking to each other properly again. During much of my 30s, with me striving to get ahead on the work front and Mel spending most of her time wrapped up in the children, weekday dinners became functional experiences. Food was consumed quickly to fuel up before I returned to my emails and Mel continued with her household chores. Even worse, we would often switch on the small TV in the kitchen while eating. This changed during the intense period of my illness when the television remained switched off during dinner, and conversation, although heavy and depressing, returned between the two of us.

Once the depression had lifted, Mel and I made the conscious decision to always eat together, never have the TV on at dinnertime, and talk to one another about all things, both major and minor. It doesn't sound very groundbreaking, does it? Isn't that just what "normal" couples do? But it was important for both of us to draw lessons from what had happened. Our marriage had certainly never been in trouble, but we had been in danger of becoming disconnected from one another, following different trajectories, drifting further apart. It was not so much a question of rebuilding our relationship, but more one of reigniting it.

It was so joyous spending time chatting about the children, deciding what little projects we might want to kickstart in the house, planning where we might go on our next holiday. Wonderfully light conversations brought some balance back into our lives.

And the talking certainly helped the healing, allowing any anxieties to bubble safely to the surface. In tandem with the honeymoon period, Efexor XL, Robin the psychiatric nurse and breaking the silence, we were now in a better position to move on to the next period of our lives.

Pause for Thought

1. In concrete terms, what medical help have you put in place to help you preserve and strengthen your mental wellbeing?
2. How comfortable do you feel discussing your mental ill health with others? What, if anything, is preventing you from doing so?
3. What role does your partner/main supporter have in helping you fully restore your mental health? How has your relationship changed? What have you learned about one another?

GETTING LEGAL GUIDANCE

It's quite possible that re-entering the workplace will require you to tackle either legal or financial matters. For example, there may be a need to re-evaluate your job role, review your contract of employment, renegotiate levels of remuneration, or re-examine the small print of medical insurance policies. Stuff that certainly needs doing, but not necessarily stuff that you enjoy doing or, more importantly, are qualified to do. It's also the kind of nitty-gritty work that can be a source of stress. It certainly was for me. Every individual case will be different. This was ours, and it does contain a health warning at the end.

During late August, Mel and I needed to make some important decisions about our next steps. I had resigned over the phone to Andy at the height of my illness, just over a week before my "accident". It was clear to me that going back to Brand Learning in my previous role was not going to be in my best interests from a mental health perspective. I would not have been able to fulfil my obligations as a director at that time. Everything was still very raw. I reconfirmed my resignation.

Now it was just a question of agreeing the terms of my departure from the company. Mel and I had to confront the financial and legal documents that had been waiting patiently for our attention. Neither of us had much appetite to dive into the details. In any case, all the paperwork we had received seemed to be in order.

My two partners had offered to cover the costs of getting advice on the Compromise Agreement from a solicitor. I had been sent this to check over and sign. This is a specific kind of contract between an employer and an employee, where the latter receives a negotiated financial sum for resigning as an employee. The Compromise Agreement is linked to matters of employment only.

This is different to a Shareholders' Agreement, a binding contract between the shareholders that covers areas such as the sale or transfer of shares and the process for resolving disputes. Before my illness, I had led the development of this document, and, with input from professional advisers, the three of us had all discussed and agreed the numerous clauses contained within it. However, we had never got round to signing it.

I was now leaving the business, and one of those clauses stipulated I was obliged to sell my 33% shareholding back to my two remaining partners. However, Mel and I believed my contribution to the birth of Brand Learning and the role I played in the initial set-up of the company should be recognized. In no way whatsoever was I a "bad leaver", departing under any kind of acrimonious black cloud or setting up in direct competition. I was a "good leaver" and would remain loyal to the company for many years to come. So I asked Andy and Mhairi if I could retain a small shareholding. I felt this was the least my efforts deserved, irrespective of what was written in the Shareholders' Agreement.

However, my request was turned down. Mel and I were disappointed, but we did not argue. Our main priority at the time was not to place my mental health under any more pressure.

So I met Andy and Mhairi on the 26 August to go through the documents, I reviewed the numbers with the company's accountants, and on 6 September 2001, I signed away my share of the company.

It was a very poignant moment. The dream had just died. But at least I was alive and kicking rather than pushing up the daisies.

Many years later, the Brand Learning story had one final twist in its tale when I discovered the implications of an unsigned Shareholders' Agreement. A lawyer advised me that because it had remained unsigned, it was possible that it might not have been a legally binding document. Therefore, it was conceivable in retrospect that I might not have been under any legal obligation to sell my shares to my two partners when I did, the September after my accident. There was no hurry. I could have hung on to them until I had fully recovered or maybe negotiated a better deal than the one I had got from the net assets valuation method we had used. That was an unfortunate bit of news, to put it mildly.

I must confess I felt somewhat of a retrospective idiot, if there could be such a term. Checking out the Shareholders' Agreement at the time with an independent lawyer would have been the obvious thing to do. After all, it was the most important of all the documents. However, this did serve to teach me one painful lesson. If you need to make any important decisions during a period of mental illness, put your trust in experts who know what they are doing. This certainly isn't the time for any DIY decision-making, particularly when it comes to the letter of the law.

And if you experience anxiety, then the last thing you want is to get bogged down in tricky minefields that are likely to increase stress levels rather than reduce them. Others love getting bogged down in the details, leave it to them.

Pause for Thought

1. Which legal or financial issues need to be considered in connection with your mental illness, and more specifically with regard to your return to work?
2. How supportive have your company been as far as these are concerned?
3. If required, have you identified and appointed any relevant independent professional advisers to help you make legal or financial decisions?

RESTARTING THE "MENTAL ENGINE"

After his stress-related breakdown in 2011, António Horta-Osorio, CEO of Lloyds Banking Group, returned to work following a nine-day stint in the Priory Clinic in London. He started working with psychiatrist Stephen Pereira, who helped him develop new habits and methods to deal with extreme stress. He was at home with his family every night, stopped reading emails or taking calls between 7pm and 7am and was in bed by 10.30pm. He began eating more protein and less carbohydrates. "And I became a better person, more patient, more understanding and more considerate. It was humbling but you learn."

His stock began to soar again as Chief Executive and it soon became business as usual, albeit with some very important safety measures firmly in place. This story represents a good example of a well-managed rise to the surface, with appropriate decompression stops built in at each stage of the rehabilitation process. Horta-Osorio had the full support of his employers, who ensured that he returned to work with the full expectation that he could continue to fulfil all his considerable potential.

It was going to be important for me to solicit the support of friends, colleagues and professionals as I began tiptoeing my way back into the workplace two months after my accident.

Although I was eager to start the rebuilding process, I was also slightly nervous as to what lay ahead. Was my Big Blip really over, or was it just in some kind of cruel remission, waiting to resurface when the moment was right? I was now unemployed with financial obligations. How could I be sure that freelance work would be available for me, even though it had been promised? And if there was work on the table, would I be up for it? Would I still be able to perform in front of a class full of challenging participants?

I entered my home office, the scene of my previous suffering, to discover my work computer was no longer a man-eating lion. It was a huge relief to turn it on, process what I was seeing in front of me and start working methodically through my very short to-do list. My brain was letting me function once again. The mental engine had restarted several months after it had conked out. The breakdown was officially over.

It was October, and I felt strong enough to start earning some money. My ascent from the depths started off pretty well. Although I was no longer employed by Brand Learning, I was able to continue my relationship with them as an independent consultant, and this presented me with my first "decompression stop". I came back into the fold as a management trainer, running courses for clients I had worked with before my illness, as well as with new ones the company had acquired since – a win-win situation for both sides. I badly needed the income and Brand Learning needed my expertise on both the training and learning fronts.

The real bonus was that my passion for the job returned in spades. My enthusiasm was almost childlike. It was as if the four-month horror show had acted like some kind of surrogate sabbatical. My impaired mind had been given the opportunity not only to restabilize fully, but also to reboot and reinvigorate itself. It was raring to go.

A lot of my freelance work was now being carried out through the company I once part-owned. Although the company was growing rapidly, it was still relatively small at the time, employing only a dozen people or so. Given my background, I remained the authority on training, the "go to" person; and newcomers to the organization would often turn to me for guidance and support. They were experts in marketing, many arriving from senior roles in major companies, but most were relatively inexperienced in the art and science of capability development. This supportive and inclusive environment helped me flourish once again, and, as a result, I became mentally stronger and stronger.

However, as I look back on this period, I do have one nagging question that remains unanswered in my mind. I wonder whether I should have made a bigger effort to move up to the next "decompression stop" more quickly and take on some management responsibility within my area of expertise. The danger of not making the next step is you can get too comfortable with where you are and lose the belief that you have what it takes to make the next jump. Your mental muscles adapt to your resting point and become more and more reluctant to flex and grow. You run the risk of stagnating; stagnation leads to boredom, which in turn leads to frustration; and, before you know it, you can end up making poor career decisions. A stagnant, frustrated brain won't always be the clearest thinking one.

A Learning Director or something similar was what I had envisaged at the beginning of the Brand Learning journey, a position where I could have led the capability agenda. I would have been more qualified to do this rather than drown slowly in the worlds of finance and the law. I wrestled with this option internally and then broached the subject with Andy, now my ex-business partner, but it seemed the door for re-entry was closed shut. There wasn't too much appetite to have me back as a permanent employee at this point. To be honest, I don't blame either of my two ex-partners for their reluctance to consider this seriously. Why would they take another chance and risk what had happened before? In any case, the company was going from strength to strength, and my absence from the top table was hardly being missed.

TOM'S STORY

Learning to ride the bike again

I had a "Big Blip" in my 20s after experiencing a stressful "turnaround" role in a different country. The company looked after me very well, and their medical advisor was in touch regularly to gauge when to start discussing my return to work. After about six weeks off work and back in my home country, I met with the HR Director and a previous boss, James, to discuss my return. They had found a role in James's team for me, where I had worked earlier in my career. While I felt it was a bit of a step down, I'd be in my home country with people I knew and would be able to rebuild my confidence.

Two or three months into the role, James took me for a coffee and told me that the new CEO was putting together a project team and had asked me to be a part of it. I was nervous, as it was in a similar area to the role where I had experienced my "Big Blip", but I also felt that I wanted to "get back on the horse that threw me". The project was to be led by an experienced director. It was a high-profile project and certainly had its pressures, but he encouraged me to steadily take on greater responsibility, and eventually I came to lead the project. We completed the project on time, on budget and to great praise from the CEO, who declared us "the team to beat"! It was a very proud achievement for me, and led to a promotion leading several teams across different divisions. I was back on the bike again!

This brought more responsibility (and pressure), but the techniques I had learnt during my recovery continued to serve me well. ACT (Acceptance & Commitment Therapy) had taught me how to "un-hook" myself from unhelpful thoughts, manage challenging emotions through "expansion" and connect with the present moment.

But even as I write this now, years later, I am not sure whether that particular "decompression stop" would have been the right one to take. I couldn't fully trust my own motivations. Why did I really want "back in"? Was I still grieving the lost opportunity of running my own company, clinging on to the dream that had drifted away? The fifth Beatle looking enviously over his shoulder, witnessing the meteoric rise of the other four? Was I still living in denial that the Big Blip had really happened, and had I already carelessly forgotten the enormous pain it had caused me and everybody around me? Or was it just Winner whispering desperately in my ear: "Go on, son, just one more go"?

Two things I know for sure. Firstly, I was relieved that the depressive episode had not caused me permanent and irreversible damage. I could still function. I could still work. I could still earn money and provide for my family. But secondly, the experience of the previous 12 months had shaken my confidence to the core. I had retreated back into a shell of sorts, doing what I knew I was capable of doing before the illness struck, albeit with a renewed vigour. Professionally speaking, I was cocooned in my "safe space", and it would take me years to stick my neck out once again. Put another way, I was back riding the same old bicycle, but for now, the stabilizers were firmly in place.

Pause for Thought

If you have had a period of absence due to mental ill health, ask yourself:

1. Which decompression steps have you agreed with your employers to facilitate your return to work?
2. How confident and comfortable do you feel about your "decompression schedule"? Do you think it is designed to help preserve your mental wellbeing?
3. How confident do you feel about your future prospects in your current company? How confident are your employers in your abilities?

THE BENEFITS OF CAREER COUNSELLING

I discovered over the next 18 months that having a sounding board to help you navigate your way through the recovery process can be invaluable. As you move from one decompression stop to the next, you need somebody to provide support, hold up the mirror and ask the hard questions.

In my first full year back in the workplace, I had become more and more bullish about things, and my ambition was beginning to inch its ugly head above the parapet. There was a danger that Winner would start to dominate Worry once again. My formula for staying mentally healthy since the Big Blip was getting the balance right between the two, satisfying both their needs. But sometimes, I forgot the rule. Or simply ignored it.

I had to make sure my next decompression step was the right one. Mel had done a wonderful job of supporting me through my illness and we would continue to have many conversations around what to do next. She was now only too aware of my strengths and the areas I struggled with, but her lack of detachment persuaded me to look for somebody "on the outside". I wanted an experienced professional to guide me through the next phase of my journey. Returning to the decompression illness metaphor, what I needed was a "dive buddy", a person familiar with the steps required to help somebody ascend to the surface safely.

Dr Sue Holland had significant experience working in the corporate sector for Unilever as their Global Head of Coaching, but was now pursuing the life of independence as a coach. Her approach involved working in the present in a person-centred way, and her goal was to facilitate transformational change within the individual. It required high doses of intuition, understanding and empathy, and exceptional levels of skill in listening, questioning and appreciating. Sue possessed these attributes in abundance.

Many years later, I asked Sue what her first impressions of me were during our first session. She said:

"You showed immense openness, but this was accompanied by a sense of lostness. You seemed 'de-shackled' from corporate life and, as a result, you were vague about what the future held. You still seemed very vulnerable, and I felt you were a little bit like gossamer, a very fine material that needed to be handled with extreme care."

Underneath my bullish surface, I was still quite delicate, and memories of "that time" remained fresh and painful. Sue was not a therapist and therefore did not have the formal training required to help people who were dealing with mental illness. This meant she had to demonstrate due diligence of care. At the beginning of every session, she would always ask me where I was mentally and emotionally on a scale of one to ten. One equalled "top of the world", and ten "bottom of the pit, suicidal". Fortunately, I had stayed well clear of ten for some time now.

After a couple of sessions, we started to explore what I wanted as far as my career was concerned. She would always ask the right questions to help me explore potential avenues, but leave it up to me to decide which path to take.

She used different methods from her toolkit depending on what I brought to our conversations. On one occasion, she left me with a book to read between sessions – *Jonathan Livingston Seagull* by Richard Bach, a quirky novella about a seagull learning about life and flight. The main message of the story centred on the importance of self-discovery.

The book helped me understand I was free to choose a different route in life, one that might end up being less conventional, less corporate, and less constrained by structures and systems. I understood that Winner needed nourishing, but I was beginning to better understand how to nourish him in a way that Worry would find acceptable. Put another way, it was perfectly reasonable to have high expectations, but it was important these were the right ones, ones that could be pursued with your mental wellbeing in mind.

"Never be afraid to fall apart because it is an opportunity to rebuild yourself the way you wished you had been all along."

Rae Smith, scenic designer

By working closely with Sue, I came to the conclusion that a full-blown return to corporate life as an employee would not have been the right option for me. I wanted to make progress, to advance my career, but I realized I needed greater freedom if I was going to reach my full potential as an individual in the business world. This seagull needed to fly a little. Sue had a simple and straightforward way of helping me make difficult decisions. She was a great "dive buddy".

Pause for Thought

1. If you have experienced a stress-related illness, do you see this as an opportunity to take stock and re-evaluate your career? Do you think that you are in the right job, one that is in sync with your core personality?
2. Do you require some external support to help you ask yourself the right questions and make the correct choices?
3. Can you identify a specific person best qualified to play this role?

HELP YOURSELF

TRY COMPLETING THE MENTAL HEALTH ADVICE BUREAU CHECKLIST

The checklist below is something I would have found useful when I started back in the world of employment after my major depressive episode. I have completed it based on what I should have done with the benefit of hindsight, which, as we all know, is a wonderful thing.

The Mental Health Advice Bureau Checklist			
Area	Issue to consider	Yes/ No	Actions to take
Mental Health Management	Have you been properly advised with regards to medication and therapy?	Yes	Continue to take medication as prescribed and meet up with the psychiatric nurse.
	Is your primary carer well briefed on your recovery plan?	Yes	Review this with Mel every few weeks.

(Continued)

Area	Issue to consider	Yes/No	Actions to take
	Is your primary carer being sufficiently supported too?	No	Encourage Mel to get some counselling.
	Are you being open and honest with others about your mental illness?	Yes	Start writing a blog so that I can share my experiences with others.
Legal and Financial	Do you require any financial or legal advice linked to any aspect of your mental illness?	Yes	I need to get professional guidance around all documentation linked to employment and shareholding.
	Have you appointed one or more independent professional advisers to manage all legal and financial affairs?	No	I need to appoint an external lawyer and accountant to review all documents.
Employment	Have you worked with your company to make appropriate adjustments to the scope of your job?	Yes	I have decided to resign as a director, but will remain as a consultant.
	Have you agreed a recovery schedule with your company including the relevant decompression stops? Does this include regular check-ins and check-ups?	No	In my role as a consultant, I will arrange a monthly chat to review my progress with my two former partners.
	Are your co-workers aware of your situation?	Yes	I will continue to be open and honest around what happened.
Career Counselling	Are you in need of more long-term guidance around your career? Have you identified suitable resources to help you?	Yes	I will start looking for an experienced life coach.

WHAT TO DO

1. For each of the four areas in the checklist, answer the questions with either a Yes or a No.
2. Working closely with a friend, co-worker or family member, identify one or more actions you need to take, depending on your answers.
3. Work together to develop a realistic timetable to implement the actions you have agreed.

A COUPLE OF WATCHOUTS

A. Avoid putting yourself under pressure to complete all the actions within an unrealistic time period, as this may affect your mental health adversely.
B. Don't expect that you will always get the advice that you want to hear or that you will necessarily get the right advice – manage your expectations.

KEY TAKEAWAYS

- **Make sure that a mental health management plan is in place:** Doctors, carers, family and friends all have a role to play to help you decompress safely.
- **If necessary, get professional advice:** There might be legal/financial matters that need sorting out, and there will be experts better qualified than you to do this.
- **Ask for close support from your employers:** Work closely with management and co-workers to ensure a safe, happy and fulfilling return to the workplace.
- **Seek out career counselling if necessary:** Depressive episodes caused by work are sometimes a strong signal you are in the wrong job; use them as an opportunity to reassess and redirect your career.

7

HAPPY CAREER PLANNING

Plan a career path that matches strengths with opportunities

I view this chapter as the most important one in the entire book. That's a bold statement, I know. But if you want to minimize the "bad stress" you experience in the workplace, then, opportunities allowing, making the right choices as far as the job is concerned, the people you work with and your working environment will all play a huge role.

This chapter will focus on one key theme:

How to identify a job or career that is as fulfilling as possible, but one that reduces the risk of unwanted stress. We will borrow a framework from the corporate world to help us achieve this goal – the business planning process.

Let's talk about caged animals first.

Your immediate surroundings and your stress levels are often interconnected. In an excellent blog written by OneGreenPlanet, the author describes very vividly the stereotypical behaviours that exotic animals, farm animals and even domestic animals exhibit when they are locked up in captivity. By stereotypical, they are referring to behaviours that are "invariant and repetitive and serve no obvious function".

One of these behaviours is irregular pacing, also referred to as repetitive locomotion stereotype, and it is most commonly observed in big cats and other carnivores. When the animal begins its pacing routine in the cage, it's often easily distracted by external sights and sounds. But the longer it remains in captivity, the more detached the animal becomes from its immediate environment and the less easily distracted it becomes. At this point, it enters into a fixed trance and seems unable to change its pace or alter its gaze. This is a clear sign of both stress and distress. According to the blog, "one study showed that the median percentage of time spent pacing back and forth by captive lions was 48%, or just under 12 hours a day. That's a big chunk of the day to feel stressed. In contrast, prides of wild lions spend at least 20 hours per day resting".

The parallel with humans is that if we find ourselves stuck in working environments for long periods of time that are misaligned with our personality, then we are also likely to start exhibiting damaging behaviours, caused by stress. We begin to develop our own versions of staring into space and pacing up and down.

Fortunately, unlike animals in captivity, we generally have a choice: as long as we have access to opportunity and are blessed with a strong support network, we can make plans to keep out of the cage, or at least plan how to escape one if we find ourselves stuck inside.

MENTAL HEALTH FACTS

- Employees are 10% less happy at work than they were in 2018.
- Two in three people feel that stress follows them home.
- One in five feel that work is negatively impacting their health.
- Two in three employees are looking for a better work/life balance in new roles.
- Flexibility is a priority for new employees.

Source: Job Exodus 2020 (Investors in People)

ENJOYING THE THEORY OF EVERYTHING

I have always loved the theory of everything. I take great pleasure in playing with business models and frameworks, pulling them apart, rebuilding them, creating hybrids and trying them out. I am a theoretical tinkerer. Two by two matrices, graphs, Gantt charts, spider diagrams, pyramids and circles. I can never get enough of them. And it isn't just in my professional life that I'm addicted to theory; it runs through my personal life too. For example, I keep a notebook of tips from all the golfing and skiing lessons I have ever received. It's meticulously updated after each session and is awash with bullet points, "stick men" drawings and bits highlighted in yellow and red for extra emphasis.

"Tell me, what is it you plan to do with your one wild and precious life?"

Mary Oliver, poet

Do. Reflect. Plan. Practise. Do again. This is the learning cycle that, in my view, should underpin any attempt to acquire a new skill, either in the personal or professional arenas. My notebook represents the Reflect and Plan stages. This discipline represents best practice if you want things to stick and if you are serious about making progress. But it's hard work, it requires persistence and you don't always get things right first time.

Disappointingly, Mel and the children have always been very dismissive about my conscientious approach toward self-improvement. They have never shown any appetite to read my top tips and, to make things worse, they have taken great pleasure in mocking me and my little book. And even though neither my golf nor my skiing have made significant progress over the years, it's probably a lack of natural ability rather than my approach to learning itself that are to blame. My notebook is now "for my eyes only".

THE BALANCED BUSINESS PLAN

I realized there were frameworks I had used on my training courses in a corporate setting that, with a little bit of tweaking, could be adapted for use at a personal level. One of these was a well-known model used to help businesses plan for both the short and the long term.

Coca-Cola, Unilever, HSBC, Microsoft, GlaxoSmithKline, McDonald's, Apple, Google … every company in the world, worth their salt, will employ some version of the business planning process to help guide them across the commercial landscape. This helps them leverage their resources to exploit opportunities and counter threats in the marketplace.

A business plan is made up of different elements, all of which build on one another sequentially:

1. How would you describe the business situation from an internal and external perspective (Situational Analysis)?
2. How does this translate into strengths, weaknesses, opportunities and threats (SWOT Analysis)?
3. In broad terms, which direction should the business take, based on your SWOT Analysis? What are your big goals (Strategic Priorities)?
4. How will you achieve these goals concretely and tangibly (Actions)?
5. How will you know you have succeeded (Measurement)?

So, one day, I drafted a business plan for myself, because I reckoned that something tried and tested in the professional arena could be conveniently adapted for personal use. I couldn't afford to get things wrong again, so my natural inclination was to find a structured way of getting things right this time around. I was desperate to avoid spending any more time in stressful captivity.

What I produced was a watered-down version of a genuine business plan, holistic in nature, taking into account both my personal and professional life. I was beginning to realize that stress management and work/life balance were closely connected concepts.

So, here it is, step by step. Don't laugh, this is serious stuff. Pen and paper at the ready please.

PART 1: SITUATIONAL ANALYSIS

A Situational Analysis forces you to scan the internal and external environment in order to paint a holistic picture of the situation you are facing. In business, this provides you with the foundation for your strategic direction by identifying macro trends, customer insights, competitor data, company results, etc. Used at the personal level, I could use the Situational Analysis to do three things:

1. Conduct a self-audit of my "performance" based on my recent history.
2. Seek inspiration from role models around me.
3. Decide which career ladders to climb and which to avoid.

My self-audit: This was an honest assessment of how things had panned out in and around the period of the Big Blip. It made for some pretty ugly reading. On the work front, I hadn't enjoyed my stint as an entrepreneur, failing miserably to cover myself in glory. I'd also lost my passion for training, and was tired of the incessant treadmill of globetrotting. On the home front, I'd forgotten how to have fun and enjoy quality time with friends and family. In a nutshell, my life was off track and needed rebalancing.

When it came to highlighting my strengths at work, I had proved myself to be a natural communicator, both empathetic and supportive of others around me. I was a self-starter, able to work independently or as part of the team. My self-perceived weaknesses on the other hand had been painfully laid bare during the last couple of years: I was prone to experiencing stress under pressure, was not very decisive, or particularly skilled at managing either people or resources. I wasn't a Steve Jobs or Bill Gates in the making, that was for sure.

The net effect of all the above was that my mental health had taken a nosedive over recent years.

Getting inspiration from others: The second part of my situational analysis was seeking inspiration from role models around me, learning from others to see how their success might guide me in the right, but not necessarily same, direction.

Two people who influenced me significantly during the rebuilding process were my two ex-partners at Brand Learning. As an outsider looking in, it was fascinating to observe both Andy and Mhairi leading the company. Mhairi appeared to be completely in her element, driving the business forward with incredible stamina and an insatiable appetite for work. She had the ability to lap up and absorb any problems that arose, both minor and major, and was very commercial and strategic. She focused on her goals, and took enormous pleasure and pride in taking a small start-up all the way to a thriving international consultancy.

Andy, extremely smart and approachable, found it easy to forge strong relationships with both co-workers and clients alike. He also possessed the ability to grasp the big and the little picture at the same time. It was very clear just how proud he was of founding his own company. And rightly so. In the later years, as the business became bigger, more complex, and as it started to change direction, Andy was astute and self-aware enough to find a different environment, a new passion in the area of leadership where he could play to his considerable strengths.

KATE'S STORY

Planning for the future by going back to the past

I had a gut feeling instantly when I joined this company that something was wrong, and an "on edge" feeling started to creep into my life as I tried to keep up with the demands of the job. I was 25 and working for one of the UK's leading management consultancies, but I soon felt a disconnect between the values of the company and my own. I found no purpose or fulfilment in my job, and the increasing demands started to affect my mental health to the point where I was getting frequent panic attacks. I ended up being signed off work with stress for three months and then I handed in my notice.

I reached out to my personal contacts to set up some meetings to discuss potential options. I ended up having a series of invaluable sessions with a career coach. These helped me build my confidence, understand my strengths and personal values, and gave me a structure to explore more suitable career opportunities. After a lot of self-reflection and many conversations, I realized that at my core I am a people person, and to feel fulfilled I need to be able to help people, be challenged (in a healthy way), and work for an organization with purpose. With these factors in mind, I drew a mind map of potential career opportunities and, by a process of elimination, I came across a trainee position to become a child psychologist. I was successful in getting this job and can honestly say I have never been happier. The supreme irony is that I studied Psychology at university! I really had gone off track!

My advice would be that it is possible to find the right job, but you need to be brave to make the change you need to thrive!

What both of them taught me was the correlation between sustainable mental health and job satisfaction. Their success only came about because they appeared to enjoy what they were doing, and they were also extremely competent at it. They didn't seem to struggle with the burden of their responsibilities and always looked very comfortable in their own skins. Mhairi liked running the business. Andy enjoyed driving excellence in marketing and learning. They had found and followed their passions, and their personalities provided the perfect match.

However, here's the rub. I would reassure myself that what Andy, Mhairi and many other very capable people at Brand Learning were doing was not right for me. We were just cut from a different cloth. Their heaven was my hell and probably vice-versa. Many of them enjoyed managing resources and taking big decisions. That wasn't me. But whereas I felt completely at ease in front of 30 intellectually demanding Chinese participants running a three-day workshop on my own in Shanghai, many of my co-workers probably didn't.

So, whenever I left the Brand Learning offices in Hampton Wick after one of my frequent visits as a freelance consultant, there was always a smile of satisfaction on my face as I made my independent way home round the M25 motorway. I was experiencing that contented feeling you get when you cuddle somebody else's newborn baby for a while before handing it back to the parents, somewhat relieved that it's not yours to keep.

Deciding which career ladders to climb: According to a *Forbes* article I read, there are two types of career growth – vertical and horizontal. The former is climbing up the corporate ladder in a straight line and taking on additional managerial responsibilities along the way. This hadn't worked out for me at Unilever, where the preordained journey from trainee to Marketing Director in ten years hadn't materialized; I hadn't got past the second rung.

Horizontal career growth, on the other hand, is migrating across the organization, giving you the chance to work in new functions, encountering a cross-section of contrasting personalities, and providing the opportunity to widen your experiences in separate areas of the business. This is the ladder that needs climbing if at some point in your career you want to gain a helicopter view of the business world before taking the vertical ladder up to the top of the company. It's also the route you take if you want to sample the different functions in the company before deciding which one suits you best.

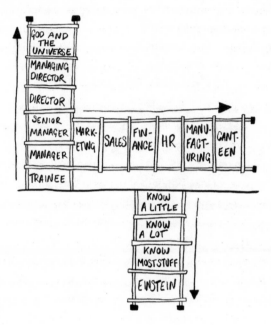

The third career ladder is the one that leads you in a different direction. Instead of progressing upwards and assuming more responsibility, or across ways where you can gain a greater breadth of experience, this path leads you down into the depths of a topic where you get the chance to become a subject matter expert – an Albert Einstein of sorts, excelling within a narrow field of focus. You become the person people turn to because you know more about the area than anybody else.

All three ladders can help you fulfil your ambitions, but in my case, it was the third I decided to climb for two different reasons. Firstly, I really enjoyed marketing training as a subject area and felt there was still so much to explore. Why not make it my ambition to become the "go to" person in this field? Winner quite liked the sound of that. And, secondly, the more knowledgeable and expert I became climbing down the ladder, the greater the sense of certainty, and the more this seemed to act like a snug mental health security blanket. Worry was definitely in favour of that.

Pause for Thought

1. How would you assess your performance on the professional front during the last three years? What's gone well, not so well? Why is that the case, do you think? Has "bad" stress or any other mental health issues affected your performance at work?
2. Can you identify any role models who seem to have got the work/life balance right? What specifically can you learn from them?
3. Do you think that you are climbing the right career ladder? What are your reasons for making this choice?

PART 2: SWOT ANALYSIS

The SWOT is probably the single most utilized tool in the business world. Its role is to synthesize the key facts that have emerged from the Situational Analysis and categorize them either as strengths, weaknesses, opportunities or threats. The first two are internal factors and the second two are external. Once you have completed the SWOT, it can be used as a springboard to help you select your strategic priorities, giving you a clear sense of direction. In short, the SWOT pinpoints where you are at and helps you decide where to go next.

Here was mine.

SWOT Analysis	
Strengths	**Weaknesses**
<ul><li>I was a very good marketing trainer.</li><li>I had a well-established professional reputation in the marketplace.</li><li>I was a creative thinker.</li><li>I was self-starting and independent.</li></ul>	<ul><li>I experienced high levels of stress.</li><li>I was not particularly skilled or decisive in the management of resource.</li><li>I could become too obsessed by work at the expense of life, often placing too much pressure on myself to perform.</li></ul>
Opportunities	**Threats**
<ul><li>Marketing capability development was a growing trend.</li><li>Brand Learning was growing quickly as a company.</li><li>Other training agencies were emerging too.</li><li>Work/life balance was becoming more important in society.</li></ul>	<ul><li>More and more individuals were leaving the corporate world to become consultants and trainers.</li><li>Mental health was still a taboo subject in society.</li></ul>

Although it makes good sense for you to have a first stab at completing the SWOT, you should ask a close co-worker or friend to give you some direct and honest feedback, particularly around your strengths and weaknesses. The temptation is to play up the former and play down the latter. Ask this person to challenge some of the assumptions you are making. Are they true? Are they really important? For example, looking at my SWOT above, was it really the case that "I was not particularly skilled or decisive in the management of resource" or was that simply my self-perception? The reason why it is so important to validate the information in each of the four quadrants is that this is the foundation for the rest of the plan; if it's wrong, the rest of the plan will take you down the wrong path.

Pause for Thought

1. What would your holistic SWOT analysis look like today? Identify three items in each quadrant.
2. Who is best qualified to validate your strengths and weaknesses from an objective viewpoint?
3. Have you carried out a comprehensive enough scan of your external environment to identify opportunities and threats?

PART 3: STRATEGIC PRIORITIES

Although the SWOT Analysis is one of the most used business frameworks, it's also one of the most misused and abused. Once completed, it's often simply "tucked away in the drawer" until the next planning period, 12 months later. So, yes, the first role of the SWOT is to itemize the most relevant strengths, weaknesses, threats and opportunities, but its second crucial job is to then do something with this information. In other words, you have to make the SWOT "sweat".

1. Which strengths will you leverage?
2. Which weaknesses will you fix?
3. Which opportunities will you look to pursue?
4. Which threats do you need to address?

Each of those four questions demand that you do something tangible with the information you have gathered. By combining, connecting and colliding elements from each of the four boxes, you can formulate a number of strategic priorities that will provide you with direction and destination.

This is how I made my SWOT "sweat":

Strategic Priorities
1. Reduce my obsession with work (weakness) and levels of stress (weakness) by achieving a better work/life balance (opportunity).
2. Leverage my skills and reputation as a marketing trainer (strength) to exploit the growing importance of marketing capability development (opportunity).
3. Avoid the responsibility that comes with managing resource (weakness) by continuing to work closely with Brand Learning as a freelance consultant (opportunity).
4. Find an avenue to leverage my creative skills (strength) by working closely with other training agencies (opportunity) and independents (threat) entering the marketplace.

The strategic priorities should provide you with a clearer overall direction on the professional front, and this clarity should contribute to the preservation of your mental health by helping lower overall stress levels in the future. Remember that your goal is to stay out of the cage.

Pause for Thought

1. What is one strategic priority on the work front for the next three years that you can identify by making your SWOT sweat?
2. What about on the personal front?
3. And which specific strategic priority can you set to help preserve your mental health?

PART 4: ACTIONS

I suspect a number of readers will be chuckling quietly now at this attempt to bring the world of business into the personal arena. And yes, at face value, it does seem a little bit over the top, I must admit. But this was how I was, how I still am today. It's my way of navigating a path through life by providing some structure.

However, I bet there are quite a few closet "theory nuts" right now, nodding approvingly. I also suspect that a number of you will shortly be investing in a little notebook and some highlighter pens. Welcome to the club.

"It's not enough to be busy, so are the ants. The question is, what are we busy about?"

Henry David Thoreau, naturalist and philosopher

Let's continue then.

Actions are the concrete execution of your strategic priorities. This is where the rubber hits the road and where the planning process becomes tangible.

In Sue's coaching sessions, one of her metaphors revolved around "banisters and rickety staircases". She wanted me to construct a strong set of personal and professional banisters that would keep me steady and stable when life became tricky: a support network, good daily habits and routines, a positive mindset, medication and therapy if required, plenty of checks and balances in place. Life would always have its ups and downs, its wobbly moments, but if the banisters remained firm, you would have something to hold on to when the stairs started creaking and squeaking. The business planning approach was part of the woodwork.

The actions listed below were how I planned to execute my strategic priorities, identified on page 143.

Actions	
Work	**Me**
• 8am to 6pm working day, limited work at weekends. • Increase expertise in marketing learning. • Remain close and loyal to Brand Learning. • Explore other alliances with agencies and independents. • Balance my professional ambition with my anxiety.	• Begin a disciplined routine of daily exercise. • Start to read more to expand my thinking. • Continue to work closely with Sue Holland (my coach). • Nourish my needs as an introvert, both at work and at home.
Family	**Others**
• Spend more quality time with Mel (and hold hands more often). • Spend more time with the kids – playing with them, watching them perform, becoming more involved with their school life. • Be mentally "present" with the family.	• Become more selective with our friendship choices. • Dive deeper into those friendships. • Always be on the lookout for others who need mental health support.

An important point to make about any planning process is that there needs to be a clear golden thread running through it from start to finish. Each phase needs to build off the last. In other words, the SWOT Analysis is a synthesis of the Situational Analysis. The Strategic Priorities are identified by making the SWOT sweat. And Actions are a tangible interpretation of the Strategic Priorities. It's important not to break the thread.

Pause for Thought

1. Translate your Strategic Priorities into a number of concrete Actions that you will begin in the next three months. Identify at least two Actions in each of the four quadrants.
2. Share these with your nominated "dive buddy" to ensure that they are concrete, measurable and achievable.

PART 5: MEASUREMENT AND REVIEW

My Happy Career Plan was implemented over the next ten years. It turned out to be a golden decade, which came to a glorious climax in 2012. For any sporting aficionados, this was an exciting year to be British. Chelsea became the first London club to win the European Champions League; Bradley Wiggins became the first British rider to triumph in the Tour de France; Europe enjoyed an astonishing comeback to snatch an unlikely victory from America in golf's Ryder Cup; Andy Murray captured his first tennis major at the US Open. And we haven't even started talking about Jessica Ennis, Mo Farah and Nicola Adams at the Olympics, or Ellie Simmonds, David Weir and Hannah Cockroft at the Paralympics.

> "However beautiful the strategy, you should occasionally look at the results."
>
> Winston Churchill, former Prime Minister

As a family, we also had a good summer. Will was now 18 and would be heading off to Manchester University after his gap year; Jack was 13 and would succeed in getting through to his secondary school of choice; and Emily found herself at the top of the podium with an outstanding set of GCSE results that enabled her to move into the sixth form with flying colours.

So, when I reviewed the "business plan" developed ten years earlier, I found myself ticking many of the boxes.

Work

My life was more balanced now. Work was mainly confined to the week and weekends were indeed the end of the working week. I picked the career ladder that went down rather than up or across. I had boosted my professional reputation as an independent marketing trainer, but had specialized even further by focusing on a specific aspect of marketing – consumer insight. I continued to maintain a good relationship with both Andy and Mhairi, and enjoyed working closely with the many highly talented people they recruited. I also spread my wings, exploring new relationships with other agencies and independents who had left corporate life.

One, in particular, was beginning to blossom. In 2008, I teamed up with a very talented marketer called Hanne Kristiansen who had just left the corporate world to pursue the life of an independent consultant. We formed a fairly loose partnership and developed a unique approach in the area of creativity, which was based on an idea conceived a few years earlier by Hanne and a co-worker at the time called Pippa Hodge. We called our little enterprise Creative Creatures.

Brand Learning and Imparta, another large agency, provided me with financial security and Creative Creatures became my "side hustle", an exciting adventure with the promise of bigger things to come. Winner and Worry were happy with the strategic direction I was taking. Success was being achieved and "bad" stress kept at bay. Happy days.

Measurement and Review score: 8 out of 10.

Me

I kept myself in pretty good shape physically. I expanded my reading repertoire, stretching my thinking in all kinds of different directions, and also made sure that my introvert gene was not put under too much pressure. This involved some delicate negotiation with Mel, who was equally keen to keep her extrovert gene well nourished. I continued my relationship with my coach Sue, pencilling in yearly MOT sessions to make sure that the banisters were well maintained. The net impact of all the above on my mental wellbeing was very positive. I remained "blip-free".

Measurement and Review score: 7 out of 10.

Family

The kitchen TV remained switched off during dinner. Mel and I talked more as a result (and not just at mealtimes) and made sure we did more things together as a couple. There was still room for improvement in the "hand-holding" department (I was beginning to suspect that our hands were incompatible). One of the things I was most pleased with was how much more time I spent with Will, Emily and Jack than I would have done without the blessing of the Big Blip. The path of independence had made this possible. I watched them play in their school matches, perform in plays, sing in musical concerts, not just at weekends but whenever I could during the week. And when I wasn't abroad on business, I was always more "present" with them at home than I had been for much of my 30s. I had managed to ditch the tag of Distant and Detached Dad. The improved relationship I was now enjoying with all members of the family was a direct result of a much more stable state of mind. And to a great extent, this could be attributed to the closer alignment between job and personality. I was a round peg in a round hole.

Measurement and Review score: 8 out of 10.

Others

Our social life improved significantly as Mel and I began to deepen our existing friendships. I remained open and available to those around me who had found themselves stuck in difficult mental places. I had acquired a heightened awareness of friends and co-workers, particularly in the business arena, who appeared jumpy or distracted, individuals who were usually quick to respond with emails but had suddenly gone missing in action. I was now more skilled at identifying the early warning signs of mental ill health in others, and I was never frightened to ask the question: "Are you alright?" Twice if necessary. I still remembered how very painful much of my Big Blip had been, and I felt a responsibility toward others whom I felt might be going down the same slippery path. And the silver lining for me was that being there for others also served to strengthen my own banisters.

Measurement and Review score: 7 out of 10.

Measurement and Review					
Work 8/10	Me 7/10	Family 8/10	Others 7/10	**TOTAL**	**30/40**

Pause for Thought

1. Which metrics will you use to help you decide whether you have succeeded in carrying out your actions?
2. How often will you sit down, ideally with a close friend or family member, and review how things are going?

As I looked back on the period between 2003 and 2012, it had been, on balance, a very satisfying decade. Room for improvement in all categories for sure, but overall it had been a solid effort all round. It would score a very commendable 30 out of 40.

Indeed, if the Simmonds family had taken part in the London Olympics in 2012, we might have won a bronze medal, based on our overall performance during the preceding ten years. Although we would have been slightly disappointed not to get either the silver or gold medal (at least Winner would have been), I could have understood the reasons why. The decade had given us only one very sad event to deal with on the personal front – the death of my mother-in-law, Lorna, who died from cancer aged 75. On the work front, my chosen career as an independent had not placed us under any real financial pressure thanks to the ample supply of training assignments I secured. So, it would be fair to say that the banisters had not really been fully tested because the staircase of life had remained pretty solid throughout.

To have any chance of winning gold, you would need to pass a much sterner test than the one I had just undergone. I had experienced a major breakdown in 2001 and all the evidence suggested I was now repaired. I was confident those repairs would be adequate if I wanted to cruise down the motorway in fifth gear for the rest of my life. But would they be strong enough to complete the Dakar Rally, travelling over 8,000km (5,000 miles) across Peru, Chile and Argentina? How would I fare travelling off-road, encountering inhospitable mountain terrain covered with treacherous rocks, sand dunes and swamps?

In other words, how would I hold up if life threw me a really nasty curve ball?

I was now going to find out whether the repairs were adequate or not, because everything would change in the autumn of 2012. Our lives would get turned upside down and we would spend the next six years in the trenches, dealing with matters of life and death.

This time, the source of my stress was not going to be the workplace. It was going to be on the home front that the banisters would get their sternest test yet. And this would be a cage from which it would be much more difficult to escape.

HELP YOURSELF

DEVELOP YOUR VERY OWN HAPPY CAREER PLAN

I am going to leave you with the template I have used throughout this chapter. At each of the different stages, I have included a question or two that will provide you with some guidance. Think hard about what you write in the boxes to avoid this becoming a template-filling exercise. It may be helpful to refer back to my example earlier in this chapter.

Situational Analysis		
Conducting a self-audit	**Getting inspiration from others**	**Deciding which career ladders to climb**
How have you "performed" recently on the personal and professional fronts?	Which other individuals can you learn from and how?	Are you best climbing the ladder that goes up, across or down?

SWOT Analysis	
Strengths	**Weaknesses**
Which are your strongest attributes, skills and competencies at work?	*Which specific "parts of your game" are not so strong and need to be worked on?*
Opportunities	**Threats**
Which trends or external events are likely to open up opportunities for you in the short, medium or long term?	*Which trends or external threats might present you and your career with possible threats in the future?*

Strategic Priorities
What would be the 3 to 5 "big things" you would like to focus on at work during the short to medium term that would help you enjoy a fulfilling career?
Which strengths will you leverage? Which weaknesses will you fix? Which opportunities will you pursue? Which threats will you address?

Actions	
Work	**Me**
Which concrete initiatives will you undertake in the workplace in the short, medium and long term?	*What do you plan to do in tangible terms to protect and nourish your own personal wellbeing?*
Family	**Others**
What can you do to improve the lives of those closest to you and enhance your relationship with them?	*What can you do to improve the quality of your relationships with friends and colleagues and make a positive difference to those in need?*

Measurement and Review				
Work /10	Me /10	Family /10	Others /10	**TOTAL /40**
How will you measure the success or otherwise of the implementation of your plan? How will you review progress? How often will you do this? What will success look like?				

WHAT TO DO

1. Decide whether you want to work either physically with paper or digitally, and construct your own business planning template. It suits me to work with the former, by finding some wall space and using a bunch of post-it notes.

2. Complete your Situational Analysis by accessing information from as many different sources as possible. This should feel very exploratory and will probably take the most amount of time. Remember, this information will drive the rest of the business plan.

3. Once you have completed your "business plan", ask a close friend or member of the family to provide you with constructive feedback. Demand "tough love" from them!

A COUPLE OF WATCHOUTS

A. Ensure that there is a clear golden thread running throughout your plan, from start to finish. Remember that each step lays the foundations for the one that follows.

B. Keep your completed plan somewhere accessible and don't tuck it away in a drawer, never to see the light of day again. This should not be an academic exercise!

KEY TAKEAWAYS

- If you want to preserve your mental health during your career, it's important that you "stay out of the cage" for as long as possible. You will have to work hard to do so.
- The business planning approach helps companies grow and remain in good financial health. You can use this framework personally, with the same objectives in mind.
- If you are going to complete a meaningful business plan for yourself, then it will require a great deal of self-awareness and honesty, as well as input from friends or family to validate the information that feeds it.

8

THE RESILIENCE MUSCLE

Embrace difficult challenges to build your inner strength

Resilience has been the real buzzword in the corporate arena during the last ten years. While this chapter will examine the concept, the inspiration for the chapter (and, in fact, for the rest of the book) came not from the workplace but from the home.

I will cover two main themes:

1. **The gift of resilience:** Everybody is born with the "resilience muscle". Difficult challenges require it when the going gets tough, and it has a far better chance  of being unleashed if those challenges have real purpose and mean something to you.
2. **The theory of relativity:** By working hard to overcome the toughest of challenges, it's often easier to cope with the stress of subsequent challenges by drawing from the well of stored resilience.

Let's begin by drawing a lesson from a very wise and courageous man.

Viktor Emil Frankl was an Austrian neurologist and psychiatrist. He was also a Holocaust survivor. He devoted most of his life to understanding the meaning of "meaning". The book for which he is most famous, *Man's Search for Meaning*, provides a graphic account of how he managed to survive the horrors of the Holocaust by finding a positive way of relating to his experiences. He noticed that it was the prisoners who were prepared to comfort others in greater need, the ones who would willingly give away their last morsel of stale bread, who survived the longest. Frankl himself volunteered to help out at the typhus ward and set up a suicide watch scheme, protecting the most vulnerable from the turmoil of their own minds. On the other hand, those who allowed the camp surroundings to destroy their inner belief systems, who couldn't find purpose in their terrible predicament, were the ones who fell victim fastest. Frankl summed things up perfectly: "If there is meaning in life at all, then there must be meaning in suffering."

"If you are going through hell, keep going."

Winston Churchill, former Prime Minister

Frankl's story is the perfect illustration of resilience in action under the most challenging of circumstances. He has also found a way of drawing some conclusions from his experiences for the benefit of the world at large.

Hopefully, very few of us will ever be unfortunate enough to endure anything as horrific as the situation Frankl and his fellow prisoners found themselves in during the Holocaust. However, we are all likely to be confronted by at least one major challenge in our lives when our powers of resilience will be tested to the limit. Whether it is the death of a close family member, a period of chronic ill health, redundancy or financial hardship. These periods can shape our future lives to a greater or lesser degree.

A TEST OF OUR RESILIENCE

I would now like to take a short diversion to share one of the biggest challenges I have faced. I say "challenges", but it felt more like a war.

On 5 May 2012, our daughter, Emily, turned 16. She was just a regular teenager going through the ups and downs of adolescence. In September of that year, she entered the sixth form at Aylesbury High School to begin her A-Levels. A month later, Mel came into my study at home with a worried look and said: "We need to talk about Em."

Emily had been making herself sick. One of her friends had become suspicious of her behaviour, had shared this with her own mother, and they had both confronted Emily. They encouraged her to speak to Mel and said that if she didn't, they felt they had no choice but to tell her themselves. They were both very concerned about Emily and were only acting in her best interests. Our daughter came home and opened up. She had developed an eating disorder.

Our initial reaction was low-key. Give it two or three months, I felt, and she would be as right as rain. I remember Mel being less certain. Six years later, as we sat with Emily at a restaurant on the island of Mallorca and watched her eating a plate full of food like any other young adult, I looked at her and told her how proud I was she was finally eating normally again. Six long years.

THE ENEMY

Anorexia nervosa is an eating disorder, characterized by an aversion to food and drink. This results in low weight and a fear of gaining weight and this food restriction is often driven by a desire to be thin. However, it is fundamentally a mental illness. Anorexia has the highest mortality rate of any psychiatric disorder.

During the next few years, Mel and I would discover what a brutal, relentless and unforgiving enemy we were up against. We would come to realize that its single-minded objective is to kill its victim and it is prepared to go to any lengths to achieve this goal.

By the end of February 2013, Mel had become a full-time carer for Emily at home with the support of the local Child and Adolescent Mental Health Services team (CAMHS). I was still working flat out to keep the money coming in, so my role was part-time. Between us, Mel and I would supervise meals six times a day, seven days a week. Emily's weight still continued to drop and pressure levels in the house continued to rise. She was now clinically depressed as a result of her desperate and exhausting struggle to keep anorexia out of her life. She was already fighting a losing battle.

Ana (the ironic term of affection we gave the illness) possessed a variety of weapons in her armoury. Here were a few. She taught Emily how to conceal food down her bra or in her socks at mealtimes, regurgitate the food she had just eaten and flush it down the toilet to lose unwanted calories. Our daughter used laxatives to ensure her bowels remained permanently empty, exercised in secret to shed more weight and filled herself up with water at weekly weigh-ins to give everyone the misleading impression she was gaining weight. And if all else failed, Emily simply refused to eat and stormed out of the kitchen like a sulky kid who stops playing when things start getting difficult. The weight continued to drop.

BUILDING MY OWN WEAPON ARSENAL

Once I realized we were in it for the long haul, I resigned myself to the fact that, once again, I would have to live with depression on the doorstep. This time it was Emily's rather than mine.

Fortunately, I was able to tap into my previous experiences of mental ill health and appeal to Emily's emotional mindset. I would sit down with her on her bed, hold her hand, ask her how she was feeling, listen carefully to what she said, empathize and remain non-judgemental. I would reassure her the "real Emily" was in hibernation, but when she emerged, she would be a new and improved version. I told her to look into my eyes and asked her to trust me. At best, I knew those words only gave her a vague glimmer of hope, but that was better than nothing. I knew that speaking the language of Irrational was often the most effective way of communicating with somebody who was experiencing a major depressive episode. I had been here before.

Hugging helped too. Both of us.

But I also needed to find ways of keeping my own resilience tank topped up. I resorted to the one thing that always helped make sense of things. Theory. I was able to repurpose some of the approaches I used in my profession as a management trainer to help Emily fight Ana. I produced all kinds of checklists, Gantt charts and diagrams, but I would only ever share with Emily material I felt might inspire or incentivize her. My daughter was a visual and kinaesthetic person in terms of how she absorbed information. She was not going to pick up a 300-page self-help book on "how to beat anorexia in 90 days". That wouldn't have been her preferred learning style. She responded to post-it notes, colour, images, pictures and inspirational quotations. So, I encouraged her to develop mood boards to illustrate what life could look like when she recovered, to list all the fabulous places in the world she would visit one day, to identify exciting professions for her in the years to come. I figured that if the future could be made to look bright, this might help her to escape the grim prison of the present.

By shifting all my focus and attention on to my unwell daughter, I was also able to keep my own mental health in credit during those early skirmishes with Ana. I was discovering that caring for others in greater need, and maintaining an outer rather than inner focus, helped me take care of myself at the same time.

But by the time we got to spring 2013, Ana was beginning to get the better of us. We weren't knocked out yet, but we were on the ropes. Emily was deteriorating and her weight continued to drop. We needed reinforcements. Ana was too strong.

THE BATTLE OF THE HIGHFIELD (MAY–JULY 2013)

It was time for us to place our daughter in the hands of professionals, experts who knew what they were doing. That famous line from *Jaws*, the movie, comes to mind, when Roy Scheider sees the enormous size of the killer shark for the very first time and realizes the scale of their task: "You're gonna need a bigger boat."

That boat was the Highfield Adolescent Unit in Oxford, a state-of-the-art NHS facility for young people aged 11 to 18 with acute mental health needs. After weeks of waiting for a place at the unit, one was now available. These are some extracts from a letter written by Emily's psychiatrist at CAMHS on 2 April 2013, to the head of the Highfield Adolescent Unit:

"When I met Emily with her parents, she appeared pale and emaciated. She is a very thin teenage girl looking younger than her age. Her hair looked dry. She described feeling dizzy and tired all the time, particularly on standing up and her blood pressure is low. Emily has been reporting very intrusive and distressing voices, some linked with her eating disorder telling her not to eat and criticizing her if she has eaten anything. Emily also describes derogatory voices telling her to harm herself."

The Highfield is a superb institution staffed with psychologists, psychiatrists, nutritionists and counsellors, all trained in the treatment of eating disorders and all completely familiar with Ana's little tricks. At last, Emily was in the hands of experts on a full-time basis.

DAVID'S STORY

The bank of resilience

"If you were to choose a cancer, it would be this one. It's eminently curable." These were the words I heard when I was first diagnosed with Hodgkin's Lymphoma in September 2015. Those words, which have lived with me ever since, were intensely positive and life-affirming, despite the obvious dangers that lay ahead. It's such a fine and difficult line to tread between deluded optimism and paranoid despair, and it felt like I needed to make a conscious decision between either shrinking into the illness or stepping into the future with a positive mindset. I found it very easy to choose the latter because, as co-workers, friends and family will testify, I possess a Tigger-esque optimism that can be sometimes perceived as at best naïve and at worst dangerous! Helped by my first couple of rounds of chemotherapy, I found the challenge of recovery strangely invigorating and simply cracked on with life. Tapping into my mental reserves and looking ahead was the only pathway I could travel. I didn't really see any alternative. There was too much to lose and everything to gain.

My zest for life, both on the professional and personal fronts, has never been greater since I was given the all-clear; and the bank of resilience I accumulated through those difficult times has stood me in great stead. During the last couple of years, I have been heavily involved in a corporate buy-out which, at times, has been highly stressful. This has been particularly the case when it's involved making decisions that have affected the lives and careers of other employees. However, I honestly believe that the strength I found to overcome my cancer has given me the belief that I can deal with most things in corporate life.

We thought we were going to be okay. We weren't. Ana was again too strong for us. All the highly trained staff at the Highfield were excellent and, day in, day out, they did everything within their power to help Emily overcome anorexia. But throughout her time in Oxford, Emily remained frustratingly close to Ana. In fact they were now closer than they had ever been before. Identical twins, joined at the hip, impossible to tell apart.

So on 22 July, two and a half months after being admitted as a day-patient and having been driven just under 200 two-hour round trips to and from Oxford, our daughter was discharged from the Highfield Unit. Her weight was now exactly the same as it had been on arrival. There had been no progress. In fact, Emily had gone backwards.

Although the Battle of the Highfield had been lost, the positive news was that my mental defences were still holding firm. They had little choice. Emily was now back home full-time in Stewkley and the pressure was on again.

THE CARDINAL CLINIC CRUSADES (AUGUST 2013–MARCH 2014)

Our unwell daughter spent the rest of the summer in free fall, losing pounds week after week. Mel and I realized there was nothing we were able to do to release her from Ana's firm grip, so I proceeded to spend my "summer vacation" head down in my home office either on the phone or on my computer. My task was now to find the one person and the one institution to whom I would "award" the limited BUPA funding we had available to help turn our daughter's illness around. We were now putting all our faith in the private sector in the hope that throwing money at the problem might be the answer.

The tricky bit was the lack of clear guidance to help me make the right choice. I needed to know which psychiatrist out there was best qualified to get the job done. Who really understood anorexia better than anyone else? Who had a track record of helping anorexics restabilize? What was their success rate? You'd think there would be a table that listed the top 20 specialists in eating disorders in the UK, based on performance and results. But there wasn't. It was just down to me to trawl through every clinic's website, study every doctor's profile and look at the evidence available to help me select the right person.

After a couple of weeks of searching the internet and having several telephone conversations to get down to a shortlist, I found the right person and the right place. The doctor in question held an NHS Consultant post in Berkshire working in acute psychiatry and eating disorders, had published widely in this area of psychiatry and was currently the Medical Director at the Cardinal Clinic, just outside Windsor.

Emily would go on to spend the next seven weeks as an inpatient under the watchful and expert eyes of everybody at the clinic while Mel and I "enjoyed" some brief respite, with Ana out of the house. Unfortunately, Ana didn't really care whether she was fighting the private or the public sector. She didn't discriminate. She saw this period as another vacation in a different location, a further opportunity to test her skills against the pros.

And once again, she emerged victorious. She always had just one more clever trick up her sleeve that prevented Emily from putting on the weight she required to recover. She was a truly fearsome foe.

THE COTSWOLD CAMPAIGN
(APRIL– SEPTEMBER 2014)

Mel and I were now on to our next plan. It was the end of March 2014 and Emily had failed to make any progress at home under parental supervision. She had also failed to make any headway at the Highfield Unit in Oxford over a three-month period or at the Cardinal Clinic in Windsor across two different stays, lasting another three months in total. Emily was now just over a month shy of her 18th birthday.

On 2 April she was assessed at Cotswold House, an NHS Specialist Eating Disorders Unit in Oxford, where the plan was to admit Emily as a long-term inpatient. She now weighed 37.4kg (82.5lb) and had dropped 2.1kg (4.7lb) in under two weeks.

Our problem was there were no beds available at the Cotswold, where there was a waiting list of a month. When the consultant psychiatrist broke this news to our daughter, Emily told her she didn't know whether she could "survive for four weeks".

"If Plan A fails, remember there are 25 more letters."

Chris Guillebeau, author and entrepreneur

All the doctor could do was assure us her physical health would be monitored closely both by her GP and the CAMHS Crisis team, who were now coming in on a daily basis. If Mel and I had any concerns about her wellbeing, we should take her to Accident & Emergency. If her condition was deemed to be life-threatening, she would be admitted. In other words, we had to wait until our daughter collapsed before we could do anything. It felt like we were playing Russian roulette with her life.

Time now for some resilience. I had to do something. It was up to me. I couldn't stay in limbo any longer.

So once again, I sat down at my desk in my home office and relegated my work to-do list to a slot later in the day. One thing I'd become much better at during this period was the ability to juggle plates. There was "Emily time", "work time", "Mel time", "Jack time", as well as a bit of "me time". The last of these was not self-indulgent. It was essential for me to be able to keep my batteries charged. A walk with the dog, a pint or two in a pub with a friend, 30 minutes of bedtime reading. Mel had her survival kit too. We both had our own set of banisters.

I dived into my computer and proceeded to look up every single NHS eating disorders clinic in the UK. Over the course of the next two days, I phoned up each and every one of them. I had nothing to lose. Unfortunately, each time I managed to get through to the right person, the response I got was depressingly consistent. "We are very sorry to hear about your daughter, these must be very worrying times for you. However, we do not have any beds available at the moment. Good luck with your search." Call after call, sympathetic rejection after sympathetic rejection.

Eventually, we struck semi-lucky. A kind-hearted woman, Lynn St Louis, working at the Eating Disorders Service at the Bethlem Royal Hospital in south London, took one of my increasingly frantic calls. She heard my pleas sympathetically and explained that a bed might be coming free within the next week or so. Interestingly, Lynn went on to tell me this was the first time a father had contacted them directly. It was always somebody from the NHS, a doctor or a member of staff from the CAMHS team, but never a desperate dad.

On 9 April, a week after her first appointment, Emily's progress was reviewed at Cotswold House. She weighed 36.4kg

(80lb) – she had lost 1kg (2.2lb) in a week. There were still no beds available at the Cotswold, but she was hanging in there.

Back to the home office. Back to the list. "We are very sorry …", "Unfortunately …", "Good luck …" The same old story. More resilience required.

They say that you can wait ages for a London bus and then two suddenly come along at the same time. The following week, our luck changed for the better. During a 24-hour period, we had two bits of excellent news. Firstly, Lynn from the Bethlem Royal Hospital called to say a bed was now available and then Cotswold House informed us one had just come free in Oxford. It felt as if we had won the lottery. Euphoria is not something you usually associate with anorexia, but that was the feeling we experienced.

Emily was admitted as an emergency to Cotswold House on 16 April 2014. Her weight on admission was 34.9kg (77lb). She had lost just under 5kg (11lb) in just over three weeks. Her BMI was 13.8. This is how the consultant psychiatrist assessed the risk:

"Given Emily's poor dietary intake she is at high risk of physical decompensation, and without regular and careful re-feeding, she would be at high risk of mortality."

The plan was to monitor her dietary intake carefully, look out for any compensatory behaviours (in other words, watch out for Ana), and keep an eye on her physical parameters and bloods. If Emily was unable to complete her diet, a supplement would be added and if that failed, she would be given Nasogastric Intubation, also known as NG feeding. A thin plastic tube is inserted

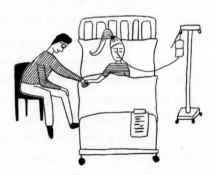

through the nose, down the oesophagus and into the stomach. Once this tube is in place, it is used to give food and medicine. After a couple of days at the clinic, Emily had a tube inserted and it remained there until she was out of the danger zone. We had found a bed in the nick of time. Bad luck Ana. Almost, but not quite. We outsmarted you this time.

Emily remained at Cotswold House for five months. Progress was slow, but it was progress, nonetheless. Our daughter gradually began to eat more and more, and slowly, ever so slowly, she started to regain weight. Pound by pound, week by week. During this period, we would make the 129-km (80-mile) round trip to Oxford several times a week. Texting became our main method of day-to-day communication, and over the months those texts became more optimistic in both content and tone.

When Emily left the unit at the beginning of October, she had reached the magical BMI number of 18.5, the minimum healthy weight. She had not fully recovered, not by a long way, but she was not at death's door.

Unfortunately, you can't stop halfway with anorexia. You either reach the summit or you risk tumbling down to the bottom. What you can't do is pitch your tent on a ledge 200 feet short of the top and hope to hang on. This is where Emily was now and where, frustratingly, she would stay for some time yet.

THE NEVER-ENDING WAR (OCTOBER 2014–2018)

Toward the end of 2014, Emily had been in Ana's clutches for over two years, but the war was far from over. We still had another four years of skirmishes to endure. During this period, Emily remained a functioning anorexic, somebody who restricts what they eat and drink so that they can maintain a weight with which they are comfortable, but they are still fundamentally unhealthy.

By the time she accepted a job as a runner working for ITV in London in her early 20s, Mel and I felt like foot soldiers who had been stuck in the trenches in a war that threatened never to end. We wore permanent looks of resignation and became weary of conversations with friends that always seemed to gravitate to the health of our daughter. However, life went on, and although Mel and I now felt slightly numbed by the events of the last few years, they had served to toughen us up. Knock back after knock back. One false start after another. Plan A, B, C, D ... But we had both managed to stay on our feet and, as a result, our resilience levels remained high.

We were going to need this when we were faced with a challenge of a different kind.

Pause for Thought

1. Can you identify one major challenge that you have faced in your life to date?
2. How did you tackle this challenge? How resilient do you think you were? What kinds of behaviours did you demonstrate?
3. What did this challenge teach you about yourself? What are some of the key learnings you can take away? What might you do differently if you faced a similar challenge in the future?

THE FINANCIAL CRISIS OF 2016/2017

During the early years of Emily's illness, my workload had fortunately been sufficient. Co-workers at both Imparta and Brand Learning, where I was still freelancing, were aware of my tricky situation at home. They remained very supportive and kept pushing work my way, so at least I didn't have to worry about paying the bills. One less thing to fret over. Dealing with Ana was still a full-time job.

However, at the beginning of 2016, this freelance work came to a grinding halt for different reasons. January of that year was the first one in my career as an independent when I earned nothing at all. Not a dime. There is always the risk when working as a freelancer that there will be peaks and troughs, so my initial reaction was that this was just a trough. Frustratingly, this trough remained a trough for month after month, and for the next couple of years we had money worries to add to our Emily worries.

I was now a 54-year-old who, by all accounts, should have been at the peak of his earning potential. Instead, I found myself at the other end of the spectrum, bringing in next to nothing. All of a sudden, I had to find a way of earning some money. I had three choices. I could either try to establish new relationships with other marketing capability agencies, or secure some regular income by returning to full-time employment. Both safe options. Or I could be a little bit more adventurous and find more imaginative ways of earning some income as an independent. I never had the intention of taking any "silly risks" again, but was there a "safe risk" option, one that could play to my strengths, while keeping me clear of dangerous territories? The answer wasn't obvious, but it was there lurking in the archives.

STRATEGIES FOR BUILDING RESILIENCE

1. **Social support:** Setting up social systems in times of crisis or trauma.
2. **Realistic planning:** Establishing realistic plans that play to the strengths of the individual and focus on achievable goals.

3. **Self-esteem:** Developing a positive sense of self-confidence, which staves off feelings of hopelessness when confronted with adversity.

4. **Coping skills:** Strengthening problem-solving skills, which help empower a person who has to work through adversity.

5. **Communication skills:** Being able to communicate clearly and effectively so that people seek support, mobilize resources and take action.

6. **Emotional regulation:** Managing potentially overwhelming emotions to help people maintain focus when overcoming a challenge.

Source: Everyday Health Resilience Resource Center

How about if I resuscitated Creative Creatures, the quirky little piece of Intellectual Property that Hanne, my business partner, and I had launched into the marketplace back in 2008? At the time, it certainly stood out within the crowd of corporate frameworks. Unfortunately, that period had also coincided with the global financial crisis, and this proved to be the wrong moment to be introducing a tool that was all about expansion and exploration when all the business world wanted to do was bunker down and cut costs. In 2013, four or five years after the launch, Hanne and I decided to put Creative Creatures on the back burner for a while. As a new mother, she wanted to dedicate herself full-time to her baby daughter. Mel and I would have to dedicate much of our time to ours, for quite different reasons.

But in 2016, large companies were starting to give more resource to the area of innovation and were looking for novel ways of achieving top-line growth. The global crisis had receded into the background, and a more optimistic outlook was emerging in many corporate boardrooms. Was the climate right for Creative Creatures to tiptoe back out into the business arena?

On a personal level, I also had to decide whether to take the safe option or give things a go just one more time. Did I have one big heist left in me? In the end, it all boiled down to what I wanted etched on my professional tombstone.

Option 1: Mark was a very good trainer who was brave once, failed, and then played it safe for the rest of his career. He retired comfortably at the age of 70.

Option 2: Mark was a very good trainer who was brave once, tried a second time, failed again, went bankrupt and spent the rest of his days living with a slightly disgruntled Mel in a caravan in the middle of nowhere.

Option 3: Mark was a very good trainer who was brave once, tried a second time, and is now living in the South of France, aged 65.

I talked things through with Mel and we decided to plump for option 3. Winner, with his receding hairline and paunch belly, was delighted by the decision, and even Worry agreed it was the right option. What the hell, you only live once – or YOLO for short.

So, I took the plunge with Creative Creatures once again. I revisited all our old business contacts, reignited cold leads, chased up warm ones, started blogging, networking, opening new doors. All the usual stuff associated with getting something new off the ground, and this included the inevitable dead ends and "thank you, but no thank you" emails that pinged into my inbox on a daily basis.

But here's the thing. I wasn't overly stressed by the unpredictability of our situation at the time or the financial insecurity that accompanied it. Although I was venturing out into uncharted waters, with no guarantee of success, I felt strangely calm and unflustered, relatively relaxed by the possibility of failure. Emily's condition was no longer acute, she was surviving day to day rather than living life to the full. However, the battle of the last few years had given Mel and me thicker skins, and this was helping us cope with continuing uncertainty both on the personal and professional fronts.

Pause for Thought

1. What words would you like written about you when you finally hang up your "corporate boots"?
2. Given your current situation, are these realistic, and is your ambition in sync with your core personality?
3. What concrete steps are you taking to ensure you merit your desired "professional epitaph"?

ENJOYING SMALL PLEASURES

This was turning out to be a surprisingly rewarding period, even though money was still scarce compared to previous years. For the first time in a career spanning two decades, we found ourselves under real financial pressure. And the timing wasn't great. Although two out of our three children had recently flown the nest, they were still all cash consumers. Of our cash, that is. So, Mel and I had to make decisions most families are forced to make from time to time. In short, we had to work out how we could earn more and where we could spend less.

We agreed to give our commercial ventures every possible chance to work out for the best, which meant a lot of my work time was spent investing in these and developing them, rather than chasing easier freelance money. As a consequence, I was working hard but not earning much.

However, we were forced to dip in to our limited savings and had the house valued just in case the downsizing option was required. Holidays were removed from the agenda. We didn't starve, but things were undeniably tight. The silver lining was that this relative austerity pushed us to find pleasure in small and inexpensive ways.

An interesting concept Mel came up with was "wet August", a slightly different take on "dry January" when you discipline yourself to go without alcohol for a whole month to purge your body of all the excesses of the festive season.

Every weekend in August, we would sit outside our house, drink in hand, and watch the sun set in the west. We were pretending to be on holiday where we had fond memories of enjoying a sundowner or two on the beach on the beautiful Greek island of Corfu. The problem was that you don't always see the sun in a typical English August, let alone see it set.

But here's the funny thing. My stress levels, in spite of the financial pressures and relative austerity, continued to remain reassuringly low. Something had changed, but I still wasn't quite sure what.

2016 and 2017 felt a bit like a sabbatical. I wasn't travelling excessively, I was busy trying to kickstart our creative venture back into life, which meant pushing myself into new areas, meeting new people, and trying out new ideas and concepts. But I also made more time available for my children and spent many hours with each of them either helping with exam revision, providing input on CVs and Personal Statements, guiding them through the job application process. It was a convenient time in all their lives for me not to be a "distant dad" flying around the globe, week in week out.

> "I am thankful for my struggle because without it, I wouldn't have stumbled across my strength."
>
> Alex Elle, author and certified breathwork coach

I just had to pretend that not earning much money was not a problem. One tactic I found useful was never asking Mel how much we had in the bank account. Just like an ostrich, I buried my head in the sand. The bad news was it couldn't remain buried there for ever and, at some point, I would have to look up and address the realities of a dwindling bank balance.

I will always be grateful that my work as a freelancer dried up during those two years. Its absence made me focus on what was really important, reassess my priorities in life and add value to those around me. Maybe it was this mindset shift that kept me mentally resilient when the pennies were short? I had discovered more purpose and meaning in the home environment.

Or maybe my stable stress levels could be attributed to something else more fundamental: The theory of relativity. Yes, we were undoubtedly under greater pressure from a financial perspective, but this pressure could not compete with what we had experienced during the anorexia wars, when the life of our daughter was on the line. Compare a dwindling bank balance or the "hardship" of a "wet August" in Stewkley with standing next to your daughter in a hospital bed, a tube inserted in her nose that was giving her the nutrients she required to stay alive. There's no comparison, is there?

Ana's "gift" to us was to provide the benchmark against which all future challenges could be measured. Somewhat ironically, she helped put things in perspective. Anyway, that's my theory of relativity. I think Einstein would have approved.

Pause for Thought

1. How "rich" is your life right now, disregarding your financial wealth?
2. Specifically, which are the positive, enriching elements and which ones are preventing you from leading a more fulfilled life?
3. What can you realistically do to increase the former and decrease the latter?

EMILY REACHES THE SUMMIT

One fine day toward the end of 2017, Emily decided that enough was enough. We had always been told that it's only when an anorexic decides for themselves that they really do want to recover completely that change will take place. Maybe Emily realized that working and living in London was only going to be possible if she was free from Ana. Maybe it was the envy of seeing all her friends moving on and up in the world. Or maybe it was just the terrifying thought of having to live with her middle-aged parents in a sleepy village in the middle of Buckinghamshire that tipped the balance. Whatever the reason, Emily started eating normally again, losing her fear of food and putting on weight.

In 2018, she went from strength to strength. We visited her more and more in London and she would take us to her favourite restaurants. Not steakhouses or pizzerias, but quirky little restaurants where vegetarian and vegan dishes were the focus of the menu. It's only parents who have endured the pain of watching their children wither away in the grip of an eating disorder who will truly understand the relief of watching them sit down with a plate of food in front of them and finish off every single morsel on the plate without a pained expression on their faces. By the end of 2018, the Anorexia Wars had come to an end. The illness had lasted six long years and during that time it had ruled our lives. We could now believe that it might not dictate the rest of them.

Our daughter had reached the top of Everest. It was time for her to soak up the view, breathe in the mountain air, and start enjoying life again.

Our challenge, as a family, had been to help our daughter win her battle against a lethal illness. My personal battle had been to fight my own demons and discover just how strong the banisters really were when the going got tough. This would all serve to define the next period in my life.

But now it was time to celebrate and have some fun. Just one final thing I need to get off my chest.

Fuck you, Ana. Fuck you.

HELP YOURSELF

COMPLETE THE RESILIENCE MATRIX

The 2 x 2 matrix opposite is a simple way of helping you identify whether what you are doing right now, work-wise, is likely to require your resilience muscle or not. I have put examples in brackets for illustration from my life/career.

Resilience Matrix

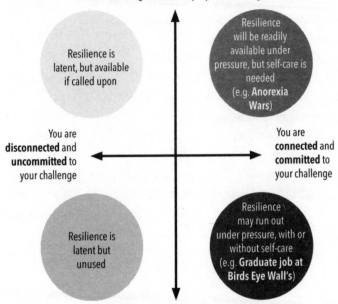

Your challenge is **HIGH** in purpose/meaning

Resilience is latent, but available if called upon

Resilience will be readily available under pressure, but self-care is needed (e.g. **Anorexia Wars**)

You are **disconnected** and **uncommitted** to your challenge

You are **connected** and **committed** to your challenge

Resilience is latent but unused

Resilience may run out under pressure, with or without self-care (e.g. **Graduate job at Birds Eye Wall's**)

Your challenge is **LOW** in purpose/meaning

WHAT TO DO

1. Plot your current job on the Resilience Matrix as well as any previous jobs you have had, including any employment as a student. You could also plot a current challenge you are facing outside of work.
2. Seek to understand in each case why you were committed/ uncommitted and why the job was either high or low in meaning.

3. If you have placed your current job in any quadrant except the top right, decide whether you are happy remaining there and, if not, what you can do to move to the top-right quadrant, if that is where you want to be.

A COUPLE OF WATCHOUTS

A. It is certainly not mandatory that all jobs must be full of purpose and meaning. It is absolutely fine if you view work simply as a means to an end. It remains your choice whether you want to operate on the right- or left-hand side of the matrix.

B. If you have placed your current job anywhere on the right-hand side, it's important to keep your banisters well oiled so that your resilience tank stays full. Ensure that you have an early warning system in place to detect the first drip, drip, drip signs of stress.

KEY TAKEAWAYS

- **The resilience muscle is innate in all of us:** The greater the purpose associated with the struggle and the more committed you are to getting through it, the more readily the muscle will make itself available. But self-care is critical at all times.

- **Understand the theory of relativity:** When you succeed in overcoming a difficult challenge in your life, you will be left with a residual build-up of resilience. This will be "available" if and when other challenges come your way.

9

THE EXPLORER'S MINDSET

Enjoy business adventures while protecting
mental wellbeing

The penultimate chapter of the book will examine some of
the factors that come into play when you start to expand your
commercial horizons, stick your neck out in the business world
and take a few calculated risks by starting something new. Are
you mentally prepared and strengthened for the challenges
ahead? Specifically, I will cover three themes:

1. **Picking the right business partners:** Finding the right people to be your soulmates on any business adventure can be a hit-and-miss affair; but it's an important choice to make, both in terms of boosting productivity and, equally importantly, maintaining mental wellbeing.

2. **Creativity and stress:** The former is unquestionably a critical element in many businesses operating within competitive landscapes, but it needs certain conditions within which to survive and thrive. In the main, stress is not good news as far as creativity is concerned.

3. **The Warrior gene:** The corporate environment isn't always a stroll in the park. Stressful conflict and confrontation often go hand in hand with ambition and the desire to succeed. You might need a warrior by your side.

But first of all, let's take a journey into space.

Can there be anything more ambitious or adventurous than taking off in a rocket and leaving planet Earth without a guarantee of ever making it back safely? Extreme exhilaration and stress in equal measures. Tom Williams, the lead scientist of the Human Factors and Behavioural Performance element of NASA's Human Research Program has developed the acronym C-O-N-N-E-C-T, which describes seven key elements required to perform safely in space.

- **C**ommunity is knowing that what you are doing has an impact on society at large. It has a purpose and meaning that goes beyond simple self-fulfilment.
- **O**penness is linked to the attributes of positivity, flexibility and creativity, all qualities that help build resilience when solving difficult problems.
- **N**etworking with family and friends on a regular basis helps the astronauts feel less separated from their loved ones on Earth, which in turn reduces feelings of isolation and loneliness.

- **N**eeds are the equivalent of the banisters – exercising, eating and sleeping well, making time for leisure activities are all "bad stress" busters.
- An **E**xpeditionary Mindset is what teams in space require in order to collaborate productively and harmoniously. Respecting different viewpoints, building consensus and resolving conflict are even more important when you can't simply pop outside to defuse any tension.
- **C**ountermeasures are what you put in place to help fortify mental strength when it finds itself under non-stop pressure. For example, writing journals to express feelings, or practising mindfulness and meditation.
- And finally, **T**raining hard for the reality of the alien environment by participating in simulations on Earth that mirror life among the stars as closely as possible.

C-O-N-N-E-C-T was developed with the adventure of space in mind, but each of the seven factors could equally apply to the adventure involved when undertaking a slightly less glamorous enterprise on Earth.

THE HOTTEST OF HOT SUMMERS

The summer of 2018 was the hottest on record in England, with average temperatures narrowly beating those seen in 1976. It will be remembered for a six-week spell from the end of June to the second week of August when it consistently reached 30°C (86°F) and the sky was a sparkling blue every single day. It was a glorious period, with countless evenings spent outside in the garden soaking up the last rays of sunshine and every Saturday and Sunday getting up bright and early simply because you wanted to be outside rather than inside.

On the work front, we were blessed with an entire convoy of London buses all turning up at the same time. Business began to boom as all the seeds we had planted during the fallow years of 2016 and 2017 started to bear fruit. Hanne, my business partner, was tiptoeing back into the business after four years of maternal hibernation and Creative Creatures was suddenly full of the joys of spring. Our small boutique agency was being engaged by some big companies: Unilever, Diageo, Colgate Palmolive, GlaxoSmithKline, and the brewing giant AB InBev. We were not just working with top-class companies and clients, but we were also getting involved in exciting projects that were stretching our creative brains in all directions.

> "A ship in the harbour is safe, but that is not what ships are built for."
>
> John A. Shedd, author and professor

And although it wasn't just about the money, Mel and I were relieved the bank balance was looking healthy again. Downsizing to release some cash was no longer being discussed. Mel was able to go back to shopping at Waitrose with confidence, and we could even afford the luxury of two short breaks abroad during the summer of 2018.

I realized the business world could be both fickle and unpredictable, and I was under no illusions our fortunes might change. Put it this way, I hadn't started looking at property prices in the South of France just yet. But this year, the corporate gods had been kind to us and both Mel's wine and my beer were flowing once again (weekends only). We weren't quite living the dream yet, but the good times seemed to be rolling once again.

COMPATABILITY MEL

The unexpected bonus in the pack as I embarked on the new crusade was Mel. To all intents and purposes, she was now becoming my second business partner.

As I headed toward the twilight of my career, I began to appreciate just how important it is, wherever possible, to partner up with people with whom there is compatibility, where each party serves not only to reinforce the value set of the other, but who also provides skills that the other doesn't have. This principle of effective collaboration can equally apply to people working closely together in an ongoing business or to individuals setting up a new business from scratch.

Steve Jobs and Steve Wozniak founded Apple in 1976. In an interview with the *Seattle Times* in 2006, Wozniak explained: "I was just doing something I was very good at, and the thing that I was good at turned out to be the thing that was going to change the world. Steve (Jobs) was much more further thinking. When I designed good things, sometimes, he'd say, 'We can sell this' and we did. He was thinking about how you build a company, maybe even then he was thinking, 'How do you change the world?'" Wozniak had the technical skills and Jobs had the business foresight. A perfect combination.

In the world of pop music, band members often adhere to the same principles of partnership by taking responsibility for different facets of the job – social, financial and creative. Not everybody is going to be good at everything. Adam Behr, Senior Lecturer in Contemporary and Popular Music at Newcastle University, writes very eloquently about one of the most famous musical partnerships of all time: "Ultimately, Lennon and McCartney complemented one another as personalities and as musicians. McCartney's melodic facility smoothed over some of Lennon's rougher edges. Lennon's grit added texture and leavened some of McCartney's more saccharine tendencies."

As Creative Creatures inched into the limelight, the amount of work began to increase significantly, and Mel started to play an increasingly important role. She got to grips with a whole bunch of important tasks that went far beyond the administrative humdrum of the back office she had been used to doing. She carried out research for articles and blog posts, assumed direct contact with key clients, and helped fine-tune and edit proposals before they went out to clients. Her confidence rose quickly the more responsibilities she took on. And while Mel loved diving into the nitty-gritty, crossing "t's" and dotting "i's", I remained a "concepts and clouds" person. We were blessed with complementary strengths.

Not only did Mel's contribution significantly increase the human resource available to the company, allowing us to explore exciting new opportunities, but, equally importantly, she was able to keep a watchful eye on my mental wellbeing. She could provide an early warning system of sorts, able to detect the first signs of "bad" stress creeping back into my life. This was always a risk as our business horizons started to expand. For quite different reasons, both Winner and Worry were kept happy, thanks to Mel.

We had been a close-knit team as far as Emily was concerned, and still were, and this bond now translated into the business world. We also succeeded in keeping fairly clear boundaries between our professional and personal lives.

However, there was one area of incompatibility that we could not resolve: hand-holding. I just need to close the loop on this. I have come to the conclusion that our hands are physically incompatible. They don't interlock properly. I blame Mel's unusually large hands. However, we have devised a four-step process that works for us. 1. Grab each other's hand; 2. Squeeze; 3. Hold, hold, hold; 4. And release. This gives us about 20 seconds of flesh contact time, which is usually sufficient to signal how much we care for one another. History tells us that both Jobs and Wozniak and Lennon and McCartney had their unresolved differences. I guess that hand-holding was one of ours.

Pause for Thought

1. Identify one person from the past or the present who has inspired you to be at your best in the workplace? Pinpoint precisely which positive behaviours they have demonstrated toward you?
2. Identify a person from the past or the present who seems to have had a negative impact either on your performance or on your mental wellbeing, or both. Why do you think that has happened? What could you have done to improve this relationship?

THE TOXIC RELATIONSHIP BETWEEN STRESS AND CREATIVITY

The financial security we were enjoying certainly took a huge burden off my mind. Stress levels remained low and, as a result, I now felt mentally liberated to be at my best. In 2018, the creative part of my brain was on fire, being bombarded with fresh and exciting ideas 24/7.

After a career spanning almost 30 years, I was now beginning to understand the relationship between stress and creativity. A little bit like oil and water, they simply don't mix.

If you find yourself trapped in a working environment swamped with never-ending to-do lists, which are jam-packed with immovable deadlines and pressure points, your neurotransmitters don't get the time and space they need to make the connections that creativity demands. But if you can find conditions where your brain is allowed to wander freely, unburdened by the frantic and the frenetic, then your creative juices will flow. Albert Einstein understood this perfectly, and that's why he spent countless hours playing the violin. By fully committing himself to something totally unrelated to his daily work routine, he was effectively allowing his subconscious to continue whirring away in the background, chewing away at a problem he had set himself. His view was that enjoying a cocktail of pastimes was highly conducive to the creative process, because this gave the brain all the fresh stimulus and tranquillity it required to create and innovate. He called this combinatorial play.

I became a convert to Einstein's philosophy on creativity because it was biologically sound, and it worked. My morning shower was not taken because I had sweated profusely overnight, but because it provided the trigger point for all my ideas to flood out after a restful night's sleep, when the subconscious had been busy combining and colliding.

"I love deadlines. I like the whooshing noise they make as they fly by."

Douglas Adams, author and screenwriter

And here is the bonus. Creativity has a positive impact on your mental wellbeing. The average human being has over 6,000 thoughts every day, which represents a big chunk of your time spent thinking. Too much of it can be a bad thing if it's not well-managed. A crowded mind that finds itself out of control can often result in stressful feelings, which in turn can serve to inflame your anxiety. Stress dampens creativity. Meditation, mindfulness and yoga have all become popular forms of therapy because their chief aim is to stop us from overthinking.

MENTAL HEALTH FACTS

The Creative Brain Under stress:

1. Creativity arises from the interaction of two large-scale systems in the brain: the default network (DN) is responsible for the generation of novel concepts through mind wandering, daydreaming, imagination; the executive control network (ECN) exerts top-down control over that generative process to select task-appropriate output.

2. In the immediate aftermath of acute stress, the ECN switches its attention to other more pressing needs like vigilance and "survival". As a result, stress will hamper the emergence of creative thought.

Source: Frontiers in Psychology

Creativity can have the same effect as meditation or yoga. When you are being creative, for example carrying out activities such as drawing, writing, knitting, gardening and certainly brainstorming in the business environment, your mind is "in the flow". It's totally absorbed with what you are doing, your heart rate slows down, and your brain is given a much-needed break from the stressful nitty-gritty thoughts of the day. Even better, the joy you are getting from the experience means that feel-good chemicals like dopamine and serotonin are released into the bloodstream at the same time. And the more of this stuff you have flowing through your body, the more stimulated you will be to continue being creatively productive.

Not only are you creating something new and exciting, but you're also doing your mental wellbeing a favour at the same time. With creativity, you get two for the price of one.

FRANKIE'S STORY

Creativity is good for your wellbeing!

For as long as I can remember, I've been interested in ceramics. My grandpa is a ceramicist and when I was growing up I loved his work, which was always on full display throughout our home. During my time at Chelsea College of Art, I was working with fabric, but really I just wanted to play with clay. The more time I spent at the wheel, the more

I realized that I wanted to make this my career. So, during the various lockdowns, I took the plunge. I started sending Frankie's Clay Club kits to children and their families, and after seeing the amazing results, I couldn't wait to invite these young creative minds into my studio. Children have such a free sense of creativity, so I wanted to capture it in clay. I then began to hold classes for adults who were looking to learn a new skill or just spend an hour immersed in clay rather than sat in front of a screen!

Pottery is not as easy as it seems, and it's always hard when someone feels disheartened by their first attempts; but persistence is key, and everyone leaves with fantastic ceramics, a smile on their face and a spring in their step. I never expected to learn so much from my students, but the teaching has taught me a great deal both about others and about myself.

Creativity lies at the heart of my wellbeing. Interacting with others and sharing a common purpose – even just for the afternoon – have helped me and my students so much in the last year. Everyone's self-confidence and self-esteem definitely seem to have been raised a notch or two!

Pause for Thought

1. How important is creativity to you either in your personal or professional life or both? Why is that the case?
2. If it is important, is it being offered conditions either at home or in the workplace that allow it to flourish?
3. Can you create any more time for leisure activities and hobbies outside of work to help you put Einstein's combinatorial play into practice?

EXPANDING YOUR PROFESSIONAL UNIVERSE

In 2018 and 2019, everything seemed possible. Having sufficient money in the bank helped, and my newly discovered allegiance to the principles of Einstein's combinatory play kept my creative juices flowing; but there were also three other fundamental factors in the picture.

Firstly, the gift of resilience. The last six years had served to strengthen this muscle significantly. The struggle against Ana had given both Mel and me strong doses of resolve, vital for the difficult and unpredictable journey that had required us to make big "life" decisions. Taking on tricky challenges in the business arena where it was "only" money at stake, was, by comparison, a walk in the park.

Emily's breakdown and subsequent repair had contributed significantly to my own repair. If you can find meaning in suffering, both your own and the suffering of others, if you can give yourself completely to somebody else in greater need than you, then this might help you emerge a stronger person. As far as I was concerned, the lessons from Viktor Frankl were spot on.

But I also continued to oil the banisters with all the usual day-to-day lubricants. I exercised plenty, rested sufficiently and socialized lots. I was always on hand to help others struggling with mental health problems of their own, and had discovered that an outward-looking perspective helps to keep you grounded at the same time. Too much introspection can be bad for your health.

I do have something important to add, however. When the going got tough, and quite a few big and unexpected events started kicking off at the same time, I asked the doctor whether I could go back on antidepressants as a pre-emptive strike. He knew my history, he agreed with my self-diagnosis, and he prescribed 100mg of sertraline a day. I have no idea what contribution they played in keeping the banisters strong but, to be honest, I didn't really care. I knew pills didn't work for everyone, and I fully intended to wean myself off them at some point, but right then I didn't want to risk upsetting the apple cart.

"When we learn how to become resilient, we learn how to embrace the beautifully broad spectrum of the human experience."

Jaeda DeWalt, author

The second factor that gave me the confidence to just "go for it" was that I was now almost 56 years old, and I refused to exit my professional career with a whimper. As long as my ambition didn't affect the health or happiness of either my family or me, I would prefer to fail gloriously rather than not try at all. Maybe I could see the Grim Reaper in the far distance and I really hoped he would grant me another 30 years or so. But, using the sporting metaphor, I wanted to make sure I didn't leave anything out on the pitch when the full-time whistle went.

In a nutshell, Worry had learnt to worry less (possibly an age thing) and Winner had learnt to operate safely within certain boundaries; although, interestingly, those boundaries had now been stretched and the playing field had been expanded to a size I had never enjoyed before. My hopes and expectations in the commercial arena were higher than they had ever been, but they now felt both realistic and achievable.

WARRIOR GENE ENTERS THE FRAY

The third factor that contributed to the expansion of my universe was a late entrant on to the genetic scene – Warrior, offspring of Winner and Worry. Warrior was a feisty little creature who really began to shake up my world. He was there to make sure I didn't get "walked all over" in the world of business. He had a firm and unshakeable understanding about what was right and wrong, equitable and just, and he wasn't prepared to back down in the heat of any battle. Warrior was the personification of resilience. A tough little cookie – probably less Attila the Hun, the barbarian who seemed to spend most of his life invading, attacking, subduing or destroying, and more Spartacus, the Thracian gladiator, who led his army of 100,000 slaves to victory against the Romans and discovered the art of guerrilla warfare.

I needed Warrior by my side, because from 2018–2020 I found myself embroiled in two lengthy disputes. Both of these ended up costing us thousands of pounds in legal fees and weeks of arguments and wrangling in an attempt to get to resolution. They were highly stressful affairs that tested our banisters to the limit. They also put my relationship with Mel under pressure as we didn't always see eye to eye, and Mel dislikes confrontation of any sort.

Before Emily's illness, I would never have contemplated getting embroiled in these kinds of conflicts. I wouldn't have had either the mental resolve or the emotional resilience to handle the stress. Things were different now because Warrior was an integral part of my make-up. I was slip-sliding toward my 60s, and I wasn't going to take "no shit from no one no more". I wasn't prepared to back down when I felt very strongly about an issue. I was happy to call out an individual or individuals if I felt I was justified. As far as resilience was concerned, I was now better equipped to suffer the fallout that would inevitably take place as a result.

The details surrounding both episodes are not important but there are some important learnings I would like to share.

Firstly, if you believe in a good cause very strongly, and this has strong meaning in your life, it is worth fighting for. If not, don't bother. It won't be worth the pain it causes. Spartacus was prepared to sacrifice his life to protect the oppressed against what he considered to be a tyrannical oligarchy; his was a moral crusade as much as anything.

Secondly, if you do end up fighting for something meaningful and purposeful, your resilience muscle will hopefully spring into action automatically, giving you the strength you need to continue with the struggle. This was what happened to Mel and me during the anorexia wars, and this is what happened in our two business disputes. But remember this. Although the muscle is innate, although it needs a good cause and a strong commitment to act, plenty of self-care is required at all times.

Thirdly, although I am definitely not suggesting you must continually be on the lookout for battles to fight, it is worth knowing that resilience, like any muscle, gets stronger the more it is used. And the more resilient you are, the better you will be able to manage any stress that emerges during challenging times.

Having said all that, I must also be clear that Warrior was somewhat of a flawed character. He needed careful supervision because his outbursts didn't always make for very pretty viewing. He didn't really appreciate the important difference between an aggressive tone of voice and an assertive one when it came to debate. It wasn't so much *what* he was saying that could be criticized, more *how* he was saying it. From time to time, I would get a disapproving text from Mel whenever she overheard me getting overheated in a business conversation in my home office.

"Tone!" was all it said.

But even though Warrior is undoubtedly in need of some mentoring and coaching, I do have a real soft spot for him. He wears his heart on his sleeve and his character fundamentally comes from a good place. He is also blessed with that innate urge to make things happen: Why not send that speculative email, make the difficult phone call or pose that tricky question. He has taught me to view rejection as an opportunity to learn, and failure as an invitation to try again.

(A footnote to all those people Warrior may have offended: while he doesn't apologize for the content of his argument or the cause for which he was fighting, he would like to apologize if the tone in which he conducted his argument was in any way offensive. He is working on his anger management.)

> ## Pause for Thought
>
> 1. How closely do you associate yourself with the concept of Winner, Worry and Warrior? Does this resonate with you?
> 2. If so, which specific characteristics do each of these possess as far as you are concerned? Which specific behaviours do they exhibit?
> 3. What do you see as their strengths? When can they have a positive impact on your life? What are the watch-outs? When do they need to be reined in to safeguard your mental health?

AND THEN OUT OF NOWHERE ...

2019 turned out to be a pivotal year. Unfortunately, my relationship with my business partner, Hanne, broke down irretrievably. To be honest, we had been accidental business partners in the first place, brought together and united by an exciting business idea back in 2008. But we lived in different countries and had always operated very independently.

When things started to take off again in 2018, we began to work more closely and that's when the cracks appeared in our working relationship. There were irreconcilable differences, and after months of trying to make things work, we agreed to go our separate ways.

There comes a point in any relationship, business or personal, when not seeing eye to eye on too many occasions can end up being unhealthy for both parties concerned. Both Hanne and I had reached that point.

On a more positive note, I had my first book, *Breakdown and Repair*, published, which told the story of mine and my daughter's mental ill health. The timing was perfect, as the topic of mental health was fast rising to the top of society's agenda. Will, my eldest son, was grinding his way through his accountancy qualifications at KPMG. Emily was continuing to progress through the ranks at ITV, loving living in London and with Ana well and truly kicked into touch. And Jack, having decided to skip the conventional path offered by a university degree, was a 20-year-old bravely exploring the world of self-employment.

We proceeded to spend a wonderful few weeks over the New Year in Australia, visiting my brother and his family. The garden was looking undeniably rosy, with everything to look forward to in the year ahead. All guns were blazing and stress levels were firmly under control.

And although things had not worked out with Hanne, I had decided to continue plying my trade in the area of creativity and training. Mel and I had invested too much time and effort during the last four years not to continue with our little adventure. It was also proving to be a lot of fun too.

So, in 2020 we took the decision to launch a brand-new agency into the market called GENIUS YOU, whose mission was to unleash the creative potential in every individual. Mel would be my new business partner. Happy days lay ahead with Winner, Worry and Warrior leading us all merrily toward our promised land.

And then out of nowhere, the world received an unwelcome visitor who would change everything for everybody.

HELP YOURSELF

TRY THE EXPLORER'S MENTAL CHECKLIST

This checklist is not exhaustive by any means, but it does ask you to consider a few questions that will help you take account of your mental wellbeing if you decide to stick your neck out in the commercial world and reach for the stars.

THE EXPLORER'S MENTAL CHECKLIST

1. Are you balancing the different requirements of both Winner and Worry in equal measures?	
2. How full is your tank of resilience? Will Warrior be able to come to the rescue when the going gets tough?	
3. Do you have plans in place to keep your banisters well oiled? Are you eating well, sleeping, exercising and socializing?	
4. Are you able to provide working conditions that will enable your creative juices to keep flowing?	
5. Are you surrounding yourself with people who can help both preserve and boost your mental wellbeing?	

WHAT TO DO

1. Carefully digest each of the five categories of questions and put either a tick or a cross against each. Be as honest as you possibly can.
2. Ask a close friend, co-worker or family member to validate where you have put ticks and crosses. Ask them to challenge any assumptions you have made.
3. Where you have placed crosses against questions, work together with your supporter to identify strategies you can put into place that will enable you to insert a tick instead.

A COUPLE OF WATCH-OUTS

A. The checklist is something you need to come back to throughout the course of your business adventure. Under pressure, it's possible that ticks will soon turn to crosses.
B. This is an inexhaustive mental health checklist, but it certainly does not represent a blueprint for commercial success. A whole bunch of questions of a

more commercial nature would have to be taken into account. For example, is there a customer need? Is your proposition differentiated?

KEY TAKEAWAYS

- **Compatibility of business partners is key:** Whether you are working on an exciting project in a big company or kickstarting a new venture from scratch, the people you work with will play a huge role in dictating its success or failure. The strength of your relationships will also either help boost your wellbeing or put a strain on it. Chemistry is very important.
- **Understand the relationship between stress and creativity:** New ventures or projects often require creative thinking in order to blossom, but they can also be accompanied by stress and pressure. Too much of the latter is not very conducive to the former.
- **New business adventures require high doses of resilience:** Going down untrodden paths and trying out things for the first time will often throw up obstacles and challenges. Having a well-behaved Warrior by your side is a must.

10

THE COVID CURVEBALL

Learn the lessons Covid-19 taught us about stress

One of the golden rules of management training is that you should never introduce any new theory during the final hours of the course. Firstly, everybody has usually checked out mentally by that point and their minds have started to focus on the journey home or the next day back in the office. And, secondly, this  is the moment to reinforce and cement the learning that has already taken place and ask the group to think how they will apply things back in the workplace. It's not the time for new news. Imagine this book has been a five-day training course. We are beginning the final afternoon. Covid-19 now makes its entrance.

The 18 months since March 2020 has been such an intense period, characterized by so much hardship and suffering all round that, unsurprisingly, mental health has become one of the main topics of conversation. And it is highly likely to remain a top priority on society's agenda for some time to come.

Each of the following four themes in this final chapter are covered in the context of Covid and will effectively summarize the book:

1. **A better understanding of your core personality:** Lockdown after lockdown, and long periods of isolation and separation from friends and family, will have served to confirm your status as an extrovert, introvert or ambivert.
2. **Work – What? Where? With whom?** The working environment is one of the biggest stressors in many people's lives. What job you do, where you carry out your work, the kind of people you work with, have all been put under the spotlight.
3. **Banisters galore:** Activities, routines, best practice habits were needed to keep the banisters firm and secure, even when the stairs became rickety during the darkest days of Covid.
4. **The beauty of constraint:** Like it or not, "bad stuff" is going to happen in your life. Both "little bad stuff" and "big bad stuff", like the coronavirus. How you reacted to the various challenges and constraints will, in part, have influenced your levels of stress. Your reaction will also have either opened or closed doors of opportunity.

But before we dissect the impact of Covid on mental health, let's revisit an amazing story of human endurance and fortitude.

After spending 69 days trapped in the collapsed San Jose gold and copper mine, 33 Chilean miners were pulled to safety, one by one, on October 13 2010, through an escape shaft barely wider than a man's shoulders. They had survived some 624m (2,050ft) underground, fending off hunger, anxiety, isolation and illness in a record-breaking feat of survival.

Here are four things that helped them pull through.

1. Nutrition: For the first 17 days, until contact was established with the surface, the miners each rationed themselves to two spoonfuls of tuna, half a cookie and half a glass of milk every 48 hours. Once they were discovered and could receive food and drink, they established a regular, nutritionally balanced meal routine.

2. Exercise: Physiologists at the surface set up obligatory schedules to keep the men physically fit, preparing them for their demanding passage up the escape shaft.

3. Communication: Once the first bore hole had established a lifeline to the men, letters, which they called "doves", began to pass between loved ones. This soon became a fibre-optic line enabling phone calls and video conferencing.

4. Sleep: A timetable of rest was put into place to maintain mood levels and establish social stability within the group.

5. Leisure: Several of the men who were soccer fanatics were able to watch live games on a small projector via a feed from the surface. Others received small music players and speakers, as well as bibles and rosaries blessed by Pope Benedict.

These five elements of day-to-day living helped preserve the physical and mental strength of the trapped miners. The same five elements play a key role in any mental health restabilization plan. And those same five elements should also have been instrumental in maintaining our wellbeing during the course of the Covid-19 pandemic.

"The human capacity for burden is like bamboo – far more flexible than you'd ever believe at first glance."

Jodi Picoult, author

NURTURING YOUR CORE PERSONALITY

The UK went into its first lockdown on 26 March 2020. There was no more socializing outside the home, drinking in pubs or gallivanting at parties. No more sporting events to watch outdoors, or shopping in the high street. No more travelling to work, and certainly no more holidays on the Costa Blanca. Effectively, many of us became prisoners in our own homes. The only consolation was that it was spring, summer was on its way and, as it would turn out, the next few months would bring some pretty decent weather.

During the first few weeks, everybody from newspaper columnists to social media users latched on to the fact that the pandemic would affect introverts and extroverts in quite different ways. As far as the former were concerned, this was "the day I have been waiting for all my life, when I am being ordered not to mix with others. Pure heaven!" As far as the latter were concerned, the government announcement was not quite so well received. "But we always go to the pub every Friday and Saturday and I have never missed a Thursday evening stroll through the shopping centre, mingling with the masses. This sounds like a version of hell to me".

Heaven for the introverts and hell for the extroverts. But is that how it panned out? Well, there was some anecdotal evidence that introverts fared better than extroverts particularly during the early stages of lockdown, their moods boosted by the absence of humanity. And, yes, if I consider my own response to this extraordinary period, I must confess that I didn't struggle too much. In fact, I would go so far as to say that I positively thrived and my energy levels had never been higher. I relished the many hours of glorious solitude spent in my small home office with only my plants for company.

And I loved the two-hour Zoom call with my friends on a Friday evening, drink and pistachio nuts to hand, because it always finished by 8pm, when my social gene had got all the exercise it needed for the day.

But, to be honest, I can't really consider myself a great test case because my working environment during Covid was not that different to how I worked pre-Covid. I had been operating happily from home for many years as an independent consultant, and the pandemic simply presented me with more of the same. However, if I had found myself stuck at home, day in, day out, surrounded by extroverted housemates, or had a young family demanding my attention 24/7, marooned in a high-rise block of flats, I don't think I would have relished the prospect of being forced into lockdown, introvert or not.

As the pandemic unfolded, the extroverts quickly found new digital ways of keeping themselves connected with family and friends. Communication apps like Zoom, Houseparty and Clubhouse became all the rage; and even though they were not providing human contact in the flesh, at least there was as much face-to-face time as needed. And if my extroverted wife was anything to go by, becoming a member of a plethora of diverse WhatsApp groups became an easy way to connect and communicate.

"The delights of self-discovery are always available."

Gail Sheehy, author

A small longitudinal study carried out on 484 US college students during their 2020 spring term revealed that as the pandemic progressed, the introverts in the group experienced increased levels of stress while their more extroverted classmates reported slight decreases. Overall, the extroverts also exhibited a marginally improved mood compared with their introverted classmates. Another study investigating the coping responses of extroverts in times of stress and crisis found that they were more likely to be able to call on problem-solving coping strategies, such as seeking emotional support.

So, in a nutshell, the verdict has not been conclusive. Neither group can claim to have held the upper hand.

Whether you are an extrovert, introvert or ambivert, the pandemic and months of lockdown would have placed you and your core personality in the pressure cooker, both on the personal and the professional fronts. Your reaction to these pressure points will have highlighted when you are at your best and when you are at your worst, which environments increase your levels of stress and which ones serve to decrease them. During the pandemic, we have all effectively been laboratory rats, part of an extensive global experiment, and it's now up to each of us to look at the evidence and draw our own conclusions.

(A quick aside. I might be wrong but I have a sneaky suspicion that my wife is slowly becoming more introverted as she gets older. I am not quite sure whether I have just managed to grind her down over the years or whether she has finally seen the light. Whatever the reason, welcome to the Land of the Loners, Mel.)

Pause for Thought

1. Has the pandemic confirmed your status as an introvert, extrovert or ambivert?
2. What kind of pressures did the pandemic put your personality under? When did you feel most stressed, and can you pin down the reasons why?
3. What has this taught you about the kind of working environments you are best suited to?

WORK: WHAT? WHERE? WITH WHOM?

The pandemic has had a brutal effect on millions of people across the world in terms of employment. In 2020, 8.8% of global working hours were lost relative to the fourth quarter of 2019, equivalent to 255 million full-time jobs. The largest labour income loss was experienced by workers in the Americas (10.3%). In the UK alone, the number of under-25s on company payrolls fell by 289,000 from January 2020 to March 2021, and there are record numbers of young people opting to stay in further education rather than look for jobs that don't exist. And although the excellent furlough scheme has protected over 11 million jobs since Covid arrived on our shores, there is still a great amount of uncertainty in the air, particularly in sectors like leisure, hospitality and travel. And with uncertainty often come pressure and stress.

However, for many people lucky enough to have retained their jobs throughout the pandemic, and even for many who have been unfortunate enough to lose their jobs, the months spent in lockdown have provided them with an opportunity to take stock, rethink and re-evaluate. Is this really what I want to be doing now and for the rest of my life? For example, in Kate's story on page 136, we discovered how a 25-year-old woman came to the conclusion that she had taken a wrong turn as far as her career was concerned. The stressful world of high-flying consultancy wasn't good for her mental welfare, and, after much soul-searching, many conversations and a lot of painstaking research, she found her calling in the world of child psychology. Kate used Covid times to seek out an occupation that gave her purpose, meaning and satisfaction.

At the other end of the career spectrum, I was a 58-year-old who had also made the decision to focus only on work that meant something to me. Covid-19 helped concentrate my mind too. Working alongside my wife, Mel, and son, Jack, we continued to commit ourselves fully to the world of creativity training. Giving individuals the confidence to believe they were creative, and providing them with the tools to build their creative muscles, felt like a really worthwhile cause. The need for creativity was only likely to increase in the months and years ahead, to help businesses find innovative solutions to the many challenges that were now popping up all over the place.

Launching our new brand, GENIUS YOU, in the middle of a (hopefully) once-in-a-generation pandemic was not ideal timing, but it was both very exciting and immensely rewarding.

MENTAL HEALTH FACTS

5,800 people were canvassed across the UK, Belgium, France, Germany, Italy, Spain and Switzerland, with the following results:

- 64% said that that their work-related stress levels had increased compared with pre-pandemic levels.
- 81% described themselves as having a "poor" or "low" state of mind.
- 82% of Britons missed physical contact with people outside their direct household.

Source: A Report on Mental Health & Wellbeing in Europe by Axa

The pandemic helped many of us reassess *what* we wanted to do as far as work is concerned. And, remember, if you are doing work you love, the chances are high that if you experience stress, it's more likely than not to be the "good" version rather than the "bad" one.

But if there was just *one* significant silver lining linked to mental health that came out of the pandemic, it was the way in which it challenged us all to think about *where* we worked best. During lockdown, we had no choice. We had to work from home.

For many, this proved to be a gift from the universe. No longer did they have to waste time commuting to and from work every day of the week, stuck on busy motorways or suffocating in crowded trains. At last, they were able to structure the working day more in line with their own personal preferences, spend more time with family, exercise more often and lead a more balanced life. However, for others, this time represented a poisoned chalice. They had always viewed the commute as a chance to wind up for the day and wind down from it, a clear demarcation between work and play. The office was a place that provided ready-made structure and routine, an opportunity to mix and mingle, and quite often a welcome break from life at home. This had now been taken away. Like the introversion/extroversion issue, this wasn't a black or white thing. There was plenty of grey.

But what lockdown gave everybody, employers and employees alike, was an extreme experience of an alternative working model. After decades and decades of sticking to the same tried-and-tested format, there was now a chance to reinvent the way in which we worked. And what quickly became known as the "hybrid model", now presented us with a unique opportunity to adopt a more balanced approach. By giving as many people as possible the chance to have some input into their choice of working environment, I believe that two clear benefits will emerge. Firstly, levels of overall productivity and creativity will increase in organizations, as people are at last able to bring their best selves to their jobs. Secondly, this freedom to choose will have a positive impact on the wellbeing of the workforce, because we'll all be better placed to avoid some of the stressors that have caused us grief in the past. How refreshing it is to hear Kevin Ellis, the PricewaterhouseCoopers' chairman, extol the virtues of the hybrid model. He is fully committed to make flexible working "the norm rather than the exception", and is already encouraging employees to work from home a couple of days a week, start as soon or as late as they like, and knock off early on a Friday!

For what it's worth, my ideal working environment is being squirrelled away in a coffee shop, with a table to myself, surrounded by a fair bit of hustle and bustle. Stimulated just enough by everything and everybody around me, but protected by the "Do Not Disturb" halo above my head. It took me over 20 years of trial and error to discover my professional oasis.

So that's the WHAT and the WHERE covered. What about the WITH WHOM?

In the twilight of my career, I finally stumbled across a business model that worked for me. Mel, Jack and I were fortunate to find ourselves surrounded by a number of talented independents, all of whom had their own small businesses and all of whom excelled at what they did. Andy Tye was a brilliant designer who was responsible for all the GENIUS YOU branding. Lucy Streule, who has drawn all the illustrations in this book, also lent her graphic design skills to the project. Mike Barrett, Sam Ellis and Pippa Dalco were all very gifted facilitators who understood both creativity and learning. And Oliver Rees was the person who led us bravely into the digital world.

Along with Mel and Jack, I often thought of us as an "Ocean's Nine" (think George Clooney and Julia Roberts), a bunch of quirky individuals with different skill sets all coming together for one final gig. An exciting adventure involving lots of hard work, twists and turns, trial and error. But with plenty of banter and laughter along the way.

"Being resilient is so much easier when you are surrounded by the right people."

Maxime Lagacé, ice hockey player

Not only was I determined to carry out work that meant something to me, not only had Covid confirmed the working environment best suited to my personality, but I also realized how important it was to collaborate with people from diverse backgrounds but who were cut from the same cloth.

Now, I fully appreciate that throughout your career you cannot necessarily choose the people you work with, but what is important is that you start painting a picture as early as you can of the kind of person who inspires you to be at your productive best. As you progress through life, this act of sifting and selecting is important, both in the personal and professional arenas. Chemistry with co-workers can be a wonderful tonic for your mental wellbeing.

Pause for Thought

1. Has the pandemic given you a different perspective on the work that you do? Are you doing a job that gives you sufficient purpose?
2. Are you now able to identify what kind of working environment will enable you to flourish? Which conditions are likely to bring out the best and the worst in you?
3. Are you now better able to appreciate the kind of people who energize you and those who tend to drain you? Are you able to migrate toward the former?

BANISTERS GALORE

If you type "Mental Health in Covid-19" into the Google search bar, unsurprisingly, you get directed to a number of websites from well-respected institutions such as the World Health Organization, the National Health Service and Mind, the UK's leading mental health charity. And each of them offer very practical, no-nonsense advice on how best to maintain mental wellbeing during the pandemic. I have been asked on numerous occasions what advice I am able to give to people who might be beginning to struggle mentally. My default top tips are the same as those of WHO, NHS and Mind: stick to the basics and make sure your banisters are securely in place. During the early stages of the pandemic, I sensed that the banisters were particularly important for professionals who suddenly found themselves in a working environment that was completely alien to them. Home.

YOU CAN'T EVER HAVE ENOUGH BANISTERS

"Self-care is not self-indulgence, it is about self-preservation."

Audre Lorde, writer and civil rights activist

Here were my top seven takeaways, based on my personal experience of lockdown:

1. **Construct your office oasis:** Create a workspace at home that you can call your own. Whether you are lucky enough to have a spare room or whether all you can secure is a small corner of the living room, personalize the space as far as possible to meet your needs. My little home office is awash with colourful pens and post-it note pads, littered with potted plants, and the walls are adorned with photos of loved ones and inspiring seascapes. This is my happy place, my bolthole.

2. **Develop a holistic timetable:** Every evening, before I shut up shop, I plan the next day, from the moment I get up to the point at which I turn off the lights at night. The plan is a balanced mix of work stuff and fun stuff. And the latter always includes tiny moments of pleasure sprinkled across the day. Romping around the garden with the dog for ten minutes, enjoying some chocolate digestive biscuits at teatime, annoying Mel (playfully) while she is trying to work. Small injections of joy are good for the spirits.

3. **Move with your mood:** Try to respect your circadian rhythms, the physical, mental and behavioural changes that affect your body and brain during any 24-hour cycle. I am in my home office for the first couple of hours of the day because that's when my mind is at its productive best. I migrate to our "Costa Kitchen" late morning to give my brain a break and enjoy some banter time with family members, my fellow lockdown inmates. I spend a bit of outside time late afternoon to let my mind wander aimlessly and give those neurotransmitters the chance to connect and collide. And finally, I have a steaming hot bath last thing at night to reward myself for a good day's work and prepare myself for a good night's sleep.

4. **Exercise as much as possible:** A gazillion people have stated that exercise is good for mental wellbeing. Why? Because it is an undisputed biological fact that exercising goes hand in hand with good mental health. You sleep better because you are more tired at the end of the day. You are happier because physical activity releases endorphins making you feel better in yourself. And your self-esteem improves because you are doing something constructive, achieving something positive. That makes it a gazillion and one now.

5. **Keep connected:** Whether you're an introvert, extrovert or ambivert, pinpoint the optimum amount of connectivity with others that works best for you. As we discussed earlier in the chapter, your mental welfare can be affected either positively or negatively by how much or how little social interaction you enjoy with others around you. Adjust the volume level accordingly, but remember that if you find yourself sliding down the slippery slope of mental ill health, open up to others around you sooner rather than later. Talk it out rather than keep it in.

6. **Disconnect from all things digital:** During the pandemic, we have, at times, never felt so isolated, and yet we have never been more connected. Zoom, Microsoft Teams, Google Hangouts, WhatsApp, Snapchat, Twitter, Facebook, LinkedIn … Where is your oasis of calm within the digital desert? What are you doing to protect it?

7. **Find your therapy:** A plethora of different therapies have emerged during the last decade or two, each designed to maintain wellbeing: meditation, mindfulness, yoga and Pilates to name but a few. I discovered the power of the 30-minute afternoon nap (aka "internal meeting") to help me relax and recharge the batteries. What's yours?

And it's one thing understanding what the banisters are, but it is another thing altogether having the discipline to cling on to them when the going gets tough. With that in mind, it's not a bad idea to identify somebody close who can act as your "banister buddy", someone who checks in with you from time to time to make sure you are still holding on firmly.

Remember, the banisters worked well for 33 courageous Chilean miners stuck underground for 69 days under the most challenging of conditions. A ringing endorsement of their value to the preservation of mental health, if ever one was needed.

Pause for Thought

1. Which banisters do you have in place to keep your mental resilience tank topped up when the going gets tough?
2. Which banisters do you want to erect or strengthen in order to provide you with additional support if required?
3. Which close friend or family member is best suited to act as your "banister buddy"?

THE BEAUTY OF CONSTRAINT

A *Beautiful Constraint*, written by Adam Morgan and Mark Barden, is one of the most powerful business books I have read. Its main premise is that the commercial world is inundated by limitations. We don't have enough budget. We don't possess sufficiently skilled human resources. Not enough time. Inadequate space. A lack of raw materials. The two authors maintain that it's how you view constraints that is all-important.

Do you see them as a burden, an excuse to shrug your shoulders, bemoan your fate, and complain to all and sundry about the unfairness of life? A victim's mindset. Or do you view them as an opportunity in waiting, the chance to find the silver lining by adopting the positive mindset of a transformer? Are you a "can't because" or a "can if" person?

I doubt very much whether the 33 Chilean miners ever dreamt they would find themselves trapped underground for 69 days. I also strongly suspect that Captain Sir Tom Moore didn't anticipate celebrating his 100th year on this planet self-isolating and protecting himself from the deadly coronavirus. And Mel and I really didn't expect to dedicate six years of our lives helping our daughter overcome anorexia nervosa. But, pardoning my vulgar language, "shit happens". And it always will happen, whether you like it or not. And with it comes constraints and challenges. The attitude you adopt to overcome them, or not, will have a direct impact on your overall state of mind.

PHILIPPA'S STORY

Frightening story with a happy ending!

Half an hour before I was due to meet up with my boss to let him know I was resigning, I collapsed at work with a thunderclap headache, blurred vision and speech. I was ambulanced to hospital with a suspected stroke. The diagnosis was Reversible Cerebral Vasoconstriction Syndrome (RCVS), a rare condition that occurs when vessels that supply blood to the brain suddenly tighten. Stress is a primary cause of RCVS.

On paper, it was a job for which I seemed to be perfectly well qualified. I had started working for a global marketing agency and was the partner in charge of Client Marketing & Capability for one of their local businesses. I had been at my previous company for ten years, and the experience I gained there, as well as my work with other organizations during my career, gave me all the skills I required. Unfortunately, that's not how things turned out. I soon found myself carrying out client-facing work that had nothing whatsoever to do with my previous experience or skill set. I was also expected to complete the work without any kind of training or guidance on how the business worked and the processes the company used. And I also felt that the way in which I was treated by those around me was disrespectful. As a result, I became increasingly stressed and my confidence took a real battering.

After spending five days in hospital, I then spent a further six months recovering from the physical and emotional toll of the experience. This was all happening in the middle of the COVID-19 pandemic. I started undertaking more daily exercise, took up Pilates and received counselling to help me get back on track. My overriding feeling now is one of immense relief. I am very excited about the future, and have just kickstarted a new business venture, working alongside some wonderful people who share similar values to my own. I wouldn't wish what happened to me on anyone, but I am beginning to view the whole experience in a positive light. A springboard to the rest of my life.

"It's your reaction to adversity, not the adversity itself that determines how your life story will develop."

Dieter F. Uchtdorf, aviator

The Chilean miners fought tooth and nail for the most precious gift of all. Life itself. And the chance to be with their loved ones once again. Captain Tom took the unprecedented step of circumnavigating his garden 100 times, supported only by his walking frame, raising an enormous amount of money for the NHS and becoming a national hero in the meantime! Mel and I buckled down to the task at hand, took on Ana and helped our daughter survive the most difficult of ordeals.

If you are able to respond to difficult obstacles with a positive mindset, it will help to reinforce your mental barricades, which will help you better respond to difficult challenges. It's a virtuous cycle.

In the *Times*, journalist Alice Thomson wrote a really interesting article, titled "How Covid kids can become Generation Grit". In spite of the chaos the pandemic has caused – the disrupted education and almost 18 months being deprived of team sport, social events and plenty of other fun stuff – Covid might end up having a galvanizing effect on the younger generation. This is particularly the case for those youngsters who have learned how to cope in lockdown and make the most of the poor hand they have been dealt. In *Past Imperfect*, a podcast series, Alice Thomson and Rachel Sylvester interviewed people who overcame traumatic childhoods and went on to achieve great success in spite of their early challenges. The survival instinct that kicks in when the going gets really tough is often the catalyst that activates the resilience muscle. It would be an interesting experiment to conduct in years to come to find out if Generation Grit really do live up to their name.

On the business front, Covid-19 certainly presented GENIUS YOU with enormous challenges. Overnight, every one of my clients announced with regret that all face-to-face training was cancelled until further notice. I was left with a stark choice: either bury my head in the sand and quickly sink without a trace, or reconfigure our offering by making our services fit for the virtual world. By choosing the latter, my horizons expanded unexpectedly to a point I didn't previously think was possible. You see, for most of my career, I have considered myself to be somewhat of a digital dinosaur, always terrified of pressing the wrong button. But by surrounding myself with the fearlessness of the younger generation, and by losing my irrational terror of mice, screens and keyboards, an exciting new universe suddenly seemed to emerge.

And even though the money wasn't exactly rolling in, both Winner and Worry were getting a big dose of what they craved: some anxiety-free adventure.

As far as I was concerned, the bonus was that by embracing constraint, not only were doors opening up that had previously been closed, but the creativity, optimism and sense of momentum that were accompanying me on the ride were all combining to fill up my resilience tank.

Earlier in the book, I claimed, tongue in cheek, to have discovered the secret of life: "As long as you are blessed with good health and a bit of luck, the route to happiness is firstly picking the right partner, secondly, choosing the right career and then sticking with both."

As I reflect back on the last 18 years, I now believe that claim to be overly simplistic. Yes, choice of partners and profession are both important, but bad stuff can still happen all around you: illness, death in the family, the thought of death, heartache, a messy divorce, austerity, friendship issues, your favourite team getting relegated, the uncertainty of Brexit, Covid-19, the certainty of nothing, middle-aged acne, molehills decimating the garden … It's how you cope with the bad stuff, both big and little, the nature of your relationship with it, and the attitude you adopt when dealing with it.

That's what counts.

Pause for Thought

1. On a scale of one to ten (where one = not at all well and 10 = magnificently) how well did you respond to the Covid-19 crisis?
2. What did you do to counter the constraints caused by Covid? What positive steps did you take to preserve your mental wellbeing?
3. Based on your learnings, if another major crisis came your way, what would you do differently this time around?

FINAL THOUGHTS

There's just one final golden principle of management training that I would like to leave you with: always end well.

The last few minutes is certainly not the time to cram in any more theory. However much they have enjoyed the course, the participants will be itching to pack up their things, say their goodbyes and inch their way toward the door. The race is run. Your objective is to ensure that every person exits the room feeling inspired, uplifted and wearing a big smile on their faces.

So, you only have time for a few motivating soundbites, one or two of which will hopefully stick.

I want to leave you with three.

SO, HOW DO YOU BEAT STRESS AT WORK?

In the Introduction, I tried to make it clear that I wouldn't be able to "cure" your anxiety. I also couldn't promise that "bad stress" would disappear from your life forever if you simply followed my magic formula. Do you remember my Roger Federer/Novak Djokovic analogy? When one beats the other on any given day, it doesn't mean they have beaten them forever. It's just that on that one occasion, they got the upper hand. And if they played each other every single day of every single year, they would both hope they would win more matches than they would lose. But neither would expect the other to disappear off the scene forever.

My goal has been to share my thoughts on how you can learn to beat stress more often than it beats you, by balancing your ambition with your anxiety. To be able to claim more victories and sustain fewer losses.

That feels more realistic.

WINNER, WORRY AND WARRIOR MARCH ONWARDS AND UPWARDS

This book remains my story, one where I have been open and honest about my actions, thoughts and feelings. I have used it to extract some lessons and learning points, but I don't want to give the impression that these are universally applicable to everybody who experiences anxiety and stress in the workplace – in no way are they a panacea. However, it would give me great pleasure if anything I have covered in the last ten chapters has resonated with you. And I would be equally delighted if you went on to apply one or two of the frameworks I have introduced to your own unique situation.

Trust me, nothing warms a trainer's heart more than seeing one of their participants actively practise something that has been preached. *So they were listening after all.*

I also don't want to give you the false impression that I currently lead a stress-free life. Trust me, I don't. I still get absurdly stressed out watching Brighton play soccer, being late for anything, others being late for me, and by a whole bunch of annoying little things. Winner and Worry have their good and bad days, and Warrior continues to have "his mad moments" from time to time. And I certainly can't claim to be this wonderfully successful businessman whose name you will soon see splashed across the annual Rich List next to the likes of Jeff Bezos, Elon Musk or J K Rowling. At this point in time, I am not even sure whether I'll be spending retirement touring the South of France or more likely eking out a meagre existence with a disgruntled Mel in a second-hand caravan in the middle of nowhere.

But I do think it is fair to say that the last few years, in particular, have given me a much more heightened awareness of my core personality, my strengths and my struggles. And right now, this enhanced understanding seems to be opening up many more doors than it is closing.

Sometimes I feel like a kid playing with his brand-new toys, refusing to put them down because he is having too much fun.

That can't be a bad thing, aged 58, can it?

MY HOPE FOR THE FUTURE

A couple of things to say before you all hit the road.

Wouldn't it just be great if, in ten years' time, society and the corporate world in particular, had a completely different perspective on people who experienced mental health issues at work? Wouldn't it be so refreshing, enlightening and liberating if they were seen as precious assets with the capacity to add significant value, rather than potential liabilities, always viewed as a burden on the business?

However, my top tip for any individual with any kind of mental illness is not to wait for that day to arrive, but to take the bull by the horns, be the best self you can possibly be, and go and do something you can be proud of.

The reason why this might be a good idea is provided by a final question and answer:

Which one word do the following individuals all have in common: Vincent van Gogh, artist; Piglet from *Winnie the Pooh*; Abraham Lincoln, American President; Lady Gaga, singer and actress; Diana, Princess of Wales; Michael Phelps, Olympic swimming champion; Oprah Winfrey, talk-show host and televison producer; Charlie Brown from "Peanuts"?

Anxiety.

Say no more.

ACKNOWLEDGEMENTS

These are the terrific people who have all helped me somewhere along the book-writing journey.

Jo and Beth from Welbeck had the foresight to see a gap in the market for a book on stress. Thank you for your faith in me. Beth held my hand throughout the process, giving me clear direction and plenty of slack in equal measure. It's been great fun! Dawn, thanks for your expert editing job, and Lucy, your illustrations will always bring a smile to my face. Mel D, the 'tough love' you provided with the early manuscripts gave me both pleasure and pain, but more of the former! I owe you much.

The following people were all very generous with their time, providing help and feedback when asked for and making sure I kept on track: Owen, Tom, Mia, Betty, Liv, Kate, Mark B, Mark H, Red Pen Shen, Andy, Alan, Anthony, Sam, Olly, Sandra, Susie, John, Rodders and Emilie.

A big thanks to the 10 individuals who agreed to contribute their own stories to the book. You know who you are! You are all stars.

Will, Em and Jack, well done for supporting your dad, and let's keep up all the banter! I am proud of you all.

And Meli: my wife, business partner, residential editor-in-chief. Thank you, thank you, thank you!

REFERENCES

Introduction

Gallup. (2021). *State of the Global Workplace*. Retrieved from https://www.gallup.com/workplace/349484/state-of-the-global-workplace.aspx. (accessed 07/09/21)

Goodreads. (2019). *Glenn Close Quotes*. Retrieved from https://www.goodreads.com/quotes/8362305-what-mental-health-needs-is-more-sunlight-more-candor-more. (accessed 22/07/21)

Health and Safety Executive. (2020). *Work-related stress, anxiety or depression statistics in Great Britain*. Retrieved from https://www.hse.gov.uk/statistics/causdis/stress.pdf. (accessed 22/07/21)

Chapter 1

Brainy Quote. (2021). Retrieved from https://www.brainyquote.com/quotes/mehmet_oz_433794. (accessed 22/07/21)

Burch, K. (2020). *Is anxiety genetic? Anxiety disorders are caused by a combination of both genes and your environment*. Retrieved from https://www.insider.com/is-anxiety-genetic. (accessed 22/07/21)

Iliades, C. (2013). *Mental Illness May Be In Your Genes*. Retrieved from https://www.everydayhealth.com/depression/mental-iillness-may-be-in-your-genes-1751.aspx. (accessed 22/07/21)

Normand, M. (2015). *College of the Pacific Faculty presentations*. Retrieved from https://scholarlycommons.pacific.edu/cop-facpres/508/. (accessed 22/07/21)

Sample, I. (2018). *'Gene map for depression' sparks hopes of new generation of treatments*. Retrieved from https://www.theguardian.com/science/2018/apr/26/gene-map-for-depression-sparks-hopes-of-new-generation-of-treatments. (accessed 22/07/21)

Therapy Group of NYC. (2020). *Does Social Media Drive Eating Disorders?* Retrieved from https://nyctherapy.com/therapists-nyc-blog/does-social-media-drive-eating-disorders/. (accessed on 23/07/21)

WebMD. (2003). *Perfectionism Linked to Eating Disorders*. Retrieved from https://www.webmd.com/mental-health/eating-disorders/news/20030205/perfectionism-linked-to-eating-disorders. (accessed on 23/07/21)

Chapter 2

Cherry, K. (2020). *The Yerkes-Dodson Law and Performance*. Retrieved from https://www.verywellmind.com/what-is-the-yerkes-dodson-law-2796027. (accessed 23/07/21)

Crawford, C. (2021). *9 Running Injuries That Can Result From The Wrong Running Shoes*. Retrieved from https://www.lifehack.org/448614/9-running-injuries-that-can-result-from-the-wrong-running-shoes. (accessed 23/07/21)

Daily-Ward, Y. (2016). Retrieved from https://www.pinterest.co.uk/pin/568509152943985294/. (accessed 23/07/21)

Flow Psychology. (2014). *Famous Extroverts*. Retrieved from https://flowpsychology.com/famous-extroverts/. (accessed 23/07/21)

Goldman, R. (2018). *5 Signs That You May Be an Introvert*. Retrieved from https://www.healthline.com/health/health-ambivert. (accessed 23/07/21)

Healthline. (2019). *What is Agitated Depression?* Retrieved from https://www.healthline.com/health/agitated-depression. (accessed 23/07/21)

Henderson, S. (2015). Retrieved from https://www.pinterest.co.uk/pin/339881103107089253/. (accessed 23/07/21)

Hopkins, A. (2015). *Star-studded Johnnie Walker campaign is brand's biggest*. Retrieved from https://www.thespiritsbusiness.com/2015/09/star-studded-johnnie-walker-campaign-is-brands-biggest/. (accessed 23/07/21)

Matthias, M. *Do Sharks Really Die if They Stop Swimming?* Retrieved from https://www.britannica.com/story/do-sharks-really-die-if-they-stop-swimming. (accessed 23/07/21)

Mayo Clinic. (2018). *Anxiety Disorders*. Retrieved from https://www.mayoclinic.org/diseases-conditions/anxiety/symptoms-causes/syc-20350961. (accessed 23/07/21)

Middlebrook, H. (2019). *5 Things to Know About Eliud Kipchoge's Attempt to Go Sub-2*. Retrieved from https://www.runnersworld.com/races-places/a28701150/eliud-kipchoge-two-hour-marathon-ineos-challenge/. (accessed 23/07/21)

Nandy, S. (2018). Retrieved from https://www.yourquote.in/saptarshi-nandy-0ap2/quotes/this-dark-sunday-night-lying-grass-staring-sky-i-wonder-get-i742i. (accessed 23/07/21)

Rampton, J. (2015). *23 of the Most Amazingly Successful Introverts in History*. Retrieved from https://www.inc.com/john-rampton/23-amazingly-successful-introverts-throughout-history.html. (accessed 23/07/21)

Scott, E. (2020). *What Is Stress?* Retrieved from https://www.verywellmind.com/stress-and-health-3145086. (accessed on 23/07/21)

Woodward, A. (2020). *Nike's controversial Vaporfly shoes are helping runners set new records, but some think it's 'technology doping'. Here's how they work*. Retrieved from https://www.businessinsider.com/why-nike-vaporfly-shoes-make-runners-faster-2019-11?r=US&IR=T (accessed 23/07/21)

Chapter 3

Adams, D. Retrieved from https://quotefancy.com/quote/960582/Douglas-Adams-He-felt-like-an-old-sponge-steeped-in-paraffin-and-left-in-the-sun-to-dry. (accessed 23/07/21)

Bombeck, E. Retrieved from https://www.goodreads.com/quotes/140315-worry-is-like-a-rocking-chair-it-gives-you-something. (accessed 23/07/21)

Cantona, E. (2003). Retrieved from https://www.azquotes.com/quote/47051. (accessed 23/07/21)

REFERENCES

Francis, G. (2016). *Britain's top 50 most annoying sounds revealed – how many of them do you make?* Retrieved from https://www.mirror.co.uk/news/weird-news/britains-top-50-most-annoying-8826311. (accessed 23/07/21)

Freeman, M. (2015). *Are Entrepreneurs "Touched with Fire"?* Retrieved from https://michaelafreemanmd.com/Research_files/Are%20Entrepreneurs%20Touched%20with%20Fire%20(pre-pub%20n)%204-17-15.pdf. (accessed 23/07/21)

Gray, R. (2017). *How flying seriously messes with your mind.* Retrieved from https://www.bbc.com/future/article/20170919-how-flying-seriously-messes-with-your-mind. (accessed 23/07/21)

Hugo, V. *Victor Hugo Quotes.* Retrieved from https://www.goodreads.com/quotes/563943-an-invasion-of-armies-can-be-resisted-but-not-an. (accessed 29/07/21)

Khalifa. W. Retrieved from https://www.azquotes.com/quote/567860. (accessed 23/07/12)

Kim S. (2016). *What really happens to your body on a flight.* Retrieved from https://www.telegraph.co.uk/travel/news/travel-advice-what-happens-to-your-body-on-a-flight-travel-health. (accessed 23/07/21)

Lewis, C.S. Retrieved from https://www.goodreads.com/quotes/241582-i-have-learned-now-that-while-those-who-speak-about. (accessed 23/07/21)

Martin, R. (2019). *What is Catastrophizing? Why is it the worst thing you could ever do?* Retrieved from https://www.psychologytoday.com/gb/blog/all-the-rage/201907/what-is-catastrophizing. (accessed 23/07/21)

Morales, J. (2020). *Two Types of Passion: Harmonious vs. Obsessive. Can passion cost you?* Retrieved from https://www.psychologytoday.com/gb/blog/building-the-habit-hero/202008/two-types-passion-harmonious-vs-obsessive. (accessed 23/07/21)

Warner, J. (2012). *The 10 Most Annoying Sounds and Why They Bother Us.* Retrieved from https://www.webmd.com/brain/news/20121012/10-most-annoying-sounds. (accessed 23/07/21)

Chapter 4

American Psychological Association. (2017). Retrieved from https://www.apa.org/ptsd-guideline/patients-and-families/cognitive-behavioral. (accessed 23/07/21)

Fry, S. Retrieved from https://www.goodreads.com/author/quotes/10917.Stephen_Fry. (accessed 23/07/21)

Guy's and St Thomas' NHS. (2016). *Abdominal breathing.* Retrieved from https://www.guysandstthomas.nhs.uk/resources/patient-information/therapies/abdominal-breathing.pdf. (accessed 23/07/21)

Mayo Clinic. (2017). *Adjustment disorders.* Retrieved from https://www.mayoclinic.org/diseases-conditions/adjustment-disorders/symptoms-causes/syc-20355224. (accessed 23/07/21)

National Health Service. *Overview - Cognitive Behaviour Therapy (CBT).* Retrieved from https://www.nhs.uk/mental-health/talking-therapies-medicine-treatments/talking-therapies-and-counselling/cognitive-behavioural-therapy-cbt/overview/. (accessed 23/07/21)

Peterson, L. (2017). *Decrease stress by using your breath.* Retrieved from https://www. mayoclinic.org/healthy-lifestyle/stress-management/in-depth/decrease-stress-by-using-your-breath/art-20267197. (accessed 23/07/21)

Rowling, J.K. Retrieved from https://www.goodreads.com/quotes/388617-depression-is-the-most-unpleasant-thing-i-have-ever-experienced (accessed 23/07/21)

Russell, B. Retrieved from https://www.brainyquote.com/quotes/bertrand_russell_103649. (accessed 23/07/21)

Schimelpfening, N. (2020). *7 Facts You Should Know About Depression. Depression Is a Real Illness.* Retrieved from https://www.verywellmind.com/depression-facts-you-should-know-1067617. (accessed 23/07/21)

Vizzini, N. *Ned Vizzini quotes.* Retrieved from https://www.azquotes.com/author/15125-Ned_Vizzini. (accessed 23/07/21)

Wiginton, K. (2020). *Physical Effects of Depression on the Brain.* Retrieved from https:// www.webmd.com/depression/depression-physical-effects-brain. (accessed 23/07/21)

Chapter 5

Angel, T. (2019). *Managing Suicidal Ideation.* Retrieved from https://www.healthline. com/health/suicidal-ideation. (accessed 23/07/21)

Atlas Obscura. (2018). *Aokigahara Forest.* Retrieved from https://www.atlasobscura. com/places/aokigahara-suicide-forest. (accessed 23/07/21)

Bernstein, R. (2016). *The Mind and Mental Health. How Stress Affects the Brain.* Retrieved from https://www.tuw.edu/health/how-stress-affects-the-brain/. (accessed 23/07/21)

Bernstein, R. (2016). *The Mind and Mental Health. How Stress Affects the Brain.* Retrieved from https://www.tuw.edu/health/how-stress-affects-the-brain/. (accessed 23/07/21)

Butler, P. (2020). *Male suicide rate hits two-decade high in England and Wales.* Retrieved from https://www.theguardian.com/society/2020/sep/01/male-suicide-rate-england-wales-covid-19. (accessed 23/07/21)

Neuroscientifically challenged. (2014). *Know Your Brain. Prefrontal Cortex.* Retrieved from https://www.neuroscientificallychallenged.com/blog/2014/5/16/know-your-brain-prefrontal-cortex. (accessed 23/07/21)

Purse, M. (2020). *What Is Suicidal Ideation? A Look at Dangerous Thought Patterns.* Retrieved from https://www.verywellmind.com/suicidal-ideation-380609. (accessed 23/07/21)

Skoutelas, C. (2017). *Think Suicide Is Selfish? Here's Why You've Got It All Wrong.* Retrieved from https://www.huffpost.com/entry/think-suicide-is-selfish-heres-why-youve-got-it_b_59223a3ce4b07617ae4cbd77. (accessed 23/07/21)

Suzuki, R. *Ranata Suzuki Quotes.* Retrieved from https://www.goodreads.com/ quotes/8399617-there-comes-a-point-where-you-no-longer-care-if. (accessed 23/07/21)

Thompson, S. (2017). *Effects of Stress on Memory and the Hippocampus.* Retrieved from https://sanescohealth.com/blog/effects-of-stress-on-memory-and-hippocampus/. (accessed 23/07/21)

REFERENCES

World Health Organization. (2021). *Suicide worldwide in 2019*. Retrieved from https://www.who.int/publications/i/item/9789240026643. (accessed 07/09/21)

Chapter 6

Caddell, J. (2020). *5 Differences Between Coaching and Psychotherapy*. Retrieved from https://www.verywellmind.com/should-i-work-with-a-psychotherapist-or-coach-2337587. (accessed 24/07.21)

Chertoff, J. (2019). *What Is Decompression Sickness and How Does It Happen?* Retrieved from https://www.healthline.com/health/decompression-sickness. (accessed 24/07/21)

CMI. (2019). *Managers not equipped to manage mental health*. Retrieved from https://www.managers.org.uk/about-cmi/media-centre/press-office/press-releases/managers-not-equipped-to-manage-mental-health/. (accessed 24/07/21)

Finews.com. (2017). Antonio Horta-Osorio. *Tablets and 16 Hours of Sleep*. Retrieved from https://www.finews.com/news/english-news/29157-antonio-horta-osorio-lloyds-burnout-2. (accessed 01/10/21)

King, M. *Martin Luther King Jr. Quotes*. Retrieved from https://www.goodreads.com/quotes/1063592-you-don-t-have-to-see-the-whole-staircase-just-take. (accessed 24/07/21)

Smith, R. *Coffee Lover Quotes*. Retrieved from https://www.goodreads.com/quotes/546525-never-be-afraid-to-fall-apart-because-it-is-an. (accessed 24/07/21)

Chapter 7

Churchill, W. *Winston S. Churchill Quotes*. Retrieved from https://www.goodreads.com/quotes/108654-however-beautiful-the-strategy-you-should-occasionally-look-at-the. (accessed 24/07/21)

Craig, W. (2016). *The Benefits of Horizontal Vs. Vertical Career Growth*. Retrieved from https://www.forbes.com/sites/williamcraig/2016/02/13/the-benefits-of-horizontal-vs-vertical-career-growth/?sh=366bd0117547. (accessed 24/07/21)

The Gazette. (2020). *Half of UK employees considering a new job in 2020*. Retrieved from https://www.thegazette.co.uk/companies/content/103466. (accessed 24/07/21)

Lamont, D. (2020). *Beyond the Zoo: How Captivity Affects the Mental Wellbeing of All Animals*. Retrieved from https://www.onegreenplanet.org/animalsandnature/how-captivity-effects-the-mental-well-being-of-all-animals/. (accessed 24/07/21)

Oliver, M. Retrieved from https://thebestbrainpossible.com/tell-me-what-is-it-you-plan-to-do-with-your-one-wild-and-precious-life/. (accessed 24/07/21)

Taylor, A. (2012). *The 2012 Dakar Rally*. Retrieved from https://www.theatlantic.com/photo/2012/01/the-2012-dakar-rally/100223/. (accessed 24/07/21)

Thoreau, H.D. *Henry David Thoreau Quotes*. Retrieved from https://www.brainyquote.com/quotes/henry_david_thoreau_153926. (accessed 24/07/21)

Chapter 8

Churchill, W. *Winston Churchill Quotes*. Retrieved from https://www.brainyquote.com/
    quotes/winston_churchill_103788. (accessed 27/07/21)

Devoe, D. (2012). *Victor Frankl's Logotherapy: The Search For Purpose And Meaning*.
    Retrieved from http://www.inquiriesjournal.com/articles/660/viktor-frankls-
    logotherapy-the-search-for-purpose-and-meaning. (accessed 24/07/21)

Elle, A. *Alexandra Elle Quotes*. Retrieved from https://www.goodreads.com/
    quotes/1177779-i-am-thankful-for-my-struggle-because-without-it-i. (accessed
    24/07/21)

Guillebeau, C. Retrieved from https://quotefancy.com/quote/1537729/Chris-Guillebeau-
    If-plan-A-fails-remember-there-are-25-more-letters. (accessed 24/07/21)

Hurley, K. (2020). What Is Resilience? *Your Guide to Facing Life's Adversities, Challenges
    and Crises*. Retrieved from https://www.everydayhealth.com/wellness/resilience/.
    (accessed 24/07/21)

Priory. Retrieved from https://www.priorygroup.com/eating-disorders/eating-disorder-
    statistics. (accessed 24/07/21)

Chapter 9

Adams, D. *Douglas Adams Quotes*. Retrieved from https://www.goodreads.com/
    quotes/731870-i-love-deadlines-i-like-the-whooshing-sound-they-make. (accessed
    24/07/21)

BBC. Retrieved from http://www.bbc.co.uk/history/historic_figures/spartacus.shtml.
    (accessed 24/07/21)

Brenner, B. (2019). *Creativity is Your Secret Advantage for Mental Health and Wellbeing*.
    Retrieved from https://nyctherapy.com/therapists-nyc-blog/creativity-is-your-secret-
    advantage-for-mental-health-and-well-being/. (accessed 24/07/21)

Cranford, N Abadie, L. (2020). *Isolation – What Can We Learn From the Experiences
    of NASA Astronauts?* Retrieved from https://www.nasa.gov/feature/isolation-
    what-can-we-learn-from-the-experiences-of-nasa-astronauts. (accessed
    24/07/21)

DeWalt, Jaeda. *Jaeda DeWalt Quotes*. Retrieved from https://www.goodreads.com/
    quotes/885119-when-we-learn-how-to-become-resilient-we-learn-how. (accessed
    24/07/21)

Popova, M. (2013). *How Einstein Thought: Why "Combinatory Play" Is the Secret of
    Genius*. Retrieved from https://www.brainpickings.org/2013/08/14/how-einstein-
    thought-combinatorial-creativity/. (accessed 24/07/21)

Pruitt, S. (2016). *8 Things You Might Not Know About Attila the Hun*. Retrieved from
    https://www.history.com/news/8-things-you-might-not-know-about-attila-the-hun.
    (accessed 24/07/21)

Shand-Baptiste, K. (2020). *Two of us: inside John Lennon's incredible song-writing
    partnership with Paul McCartney*. Retrieved from https://theconversation.com/
    two-of-us-inside-john-lennons-incredible-songwriting-partnership-with-paul-
    mccartney-147857. (accessed 24/07/21)

Shedd, A. Retrieved from https://quoteinvestigator.com/tag/john-a-shedd/. (accessed
    27/07/21)

REFERENCES

Shontell, A. (2010). *10 Super Successful Co-Founders, And Why Their Partnerships Worked.* Retrieved from https://www.businessinsider.com/10-super-successful-co-founders-and-why-their-partnerships-worked-2010-7?r=US&IR=T. (accessed 24/07/21)

Vartanian, O. Suedfeld, P. (2020). *The Creative Brain Under Stress: Considerations for Performance in Extreme Environments.* Retrieved from https://www.frontiersin.org/articles/10.3389/fpsyg.2020.585969/full. (accessed 24/07/21)

Chapter 10

BBC. (2021). *Captain Sir Tom Moore: 'National Inspiration' dies with Covid-19.* Retrieved from https://www.bbc.co.uk/news/uk-england-beds-bucks-herts-55881753. (accessed 24/07/21)

BBC. (2021). *PwC says start when you like, leave when you like.* Retrieved from https://www.bbc.co.uk/news/business-56591189. (accessed 24/07/21)

International Labour Organisation. (2021). *ILO Monitor: Covid-19 and the world of work. Seventh edition.* Retrieved from https://www.ilo.org/wcmsp5/groups/public/---dgreports/---dcomm/documents/briefingnote/wcms_767028.pdf. (accessed 08/09/21)

King, B. (2021). *Unemployment rate: How many people are out of work?* Retrieved from https://www.bbc.co.uk/news/business-52660591. (accessed 24/07/21)

Ku, L. (2020). *Have introverts really fared better in lockdown?* Retrieved from https://theconversation.com/have-introverts-really-fared-better-in-lockdown-158800. (accessed 24/07/21)

Lagacé, M. *Maxime Lagacé Quotes.* Retrieved from https://www.goodreads.com/author/quotes/19952072.Maxime_Lagac. (accessed 24/07/21)

Lorde, A. *Audre Lorde Quotes.* Retrieved from https://www.goodreads.com/quotes/437563-caring-for-myself-is-not-self-indulgence-it-is-self-preservation. (accessed 24/07/21)

Mind. *Physical activity and your mental health.* Retrieved from https://www.mind.org.uk/information-support/tips-for-everyday-living/physical-activity-and-your-mental-health/about-physical-activity/. (accessed 24/07/21)

Mind. Retrieved from https://www.mind.org.uk/information-support/coronavirus/. (accessed 24/07/21)

Morgan, A Barden, M. *A Beautiful Constraint.* Retrieved from http://www.abeautifulconstraint.com/the-book-2. (accessed 24/07/21)

NHS. Retrieved from https://www.nhs.uk/every-mind-matters/coronavirus/mental-wellbeing-while-staying-at-home/. (accessed 24/07/21)

Paton, N. (2020). *Covid-19 fuelling surge in work-related stress across UK and Europe.* Retrieved from https://www.personneltoday.com/hr/covid-19-fuelling-surge-in-work-related-stress-across-uk-and-europe/. (accessed 24/07/21)

Picoult, J. *Jodi Picoult Quotes.* Retrieved from https://www.goodreads.com/quotes/166675-the-human-capacity-for-burden-is-like-bamboo--far-more. (accessed 24/07/21)

Plos Org. (2021). *Personality trait predictors of adjustment during the COVID pandemic among college students.* Retrieved from https://journals.plos.org/plosone/article?id=10.1371/journal.pone.0248895. (accessed 24/07/21)

Reuters. (2010). Q&A: *How did Chile's trapped miners survive?* Retrieved from https://www.reuters.com/article/us-chile-miners-qa-idUSTRE69B5BP20101014. (accessed 24/07/21)

Sheehy, G. *Gail Sheehy Quotes.* Retrieved from https://www.brainyquote.com/quotes/gail_sheehy_379401. (accessed 24/07/21)

Statista. (2021). *Cumulative number of jobs furloughed under the job retention scheme in the United Kingdom between April 20, 2020, and June 14, 2021.* Retrieved from https://www.statista.com/statistics/1116638/uk-number-of-people-on-furlough/. (accessed 24/07/21)

Suni, E. (2020). *Circadian Rhythm.* Retrieved from https://www.sleepfoundation.org/circadian-rhythm. (accessed 24/07/21)

Thomson, A. (2021). *How Covid kids can become Generation Grit.* Retrieved from https://www.thetimes.co.uk/article/how-covid-kids-can-become-generation-grit-0kwllxq53. (accessed 25/07/21)

Uchtdorf, D. *Dieter F. Uchtdorf Quotes.* Retrieved from https://www.goodreads.com/quotes/1198774-it-is-your-reaction-to-adversity-not-the-adversity-itself. (accessed 24/07/21)

WHO. Retrieved from https://www.who.int/teams/mental-health-and-substance-use/covid-19. (accessed 24/07/21)

Final Words

Aloe House. *9 famous People & Celebrities With Social Anxiety Disorders.* Retrieved from https://alorecovery.com/9-famous-people-celebrities-with-social-anxiety-disorders/.(accessed 24/07/21)

Casano, A. (2020). *Cartoon Characters You Never Realized Suffer From Mental Disorders.* Retrieved from https://www.ranker.com/list/cartoon-characters-suffering-from-mental-disorders/anncasano. (accessed 24/07/12)

Cohen, L. *Leonard Cohen Quotes.* Retrieved from https://www.goodreads.com/quotes/4484-there-is-a-crack-in-everything-that-s-how-the-light. (accessed 24/0721)

Hruetic, A. (2019). *27 Celebrities Open Up about Living With Anxiety and Panic Attacks.* Retrieved from https://www.prevention.com/health/mental-health/g27609683/celebrities-with-anxiety-disorders/?slide=24. (accessed 24/07/21)

India Today. (2016). *Each Winnie the Pooh character suffers from a disorder. Do you agree?* Retrieved from https://www.indiatoday.in/lifestyle/culture/story/each-winnie-the-pooh-character-suffers-from-a-disorder-tigger-a-a-milne-cma-canadian-medical-association. (accessed 24/0721)

Mann, S. (2017). *Princess Diana 'struggled with anxiety and bulimia over relationship with Charles', new tapes reveal.* Retrieved from https://www.standard.co.uk/news/uk/princess-diana-struggled-with-bulimia-and-anxiety-over-relationship-with-charles-new-tapes-reveal-a3561806.html. (accessed 24/07/21)

Social Work Degree. (2013). *10 Famous People with Anxiety Disorders.* Retrieved from https://www.socialworkdegreeguide.com/10-famous-people-with-anxiety-disorders/. (accessed 24/07/21)

USEFUL RESOURCES

GENERAL MENTAL HEALTH RESOURCES

UK
Mental Health Foundation UK: www.mentalhealth.org.uk
Mind UK: www.mind.org.uk
Rethink Mental Illness: www.rethink.org
Samaritans: www.samaritans.org, helpline: 116 123
Scottish Association for Mental Health (SAMH): www.samh.org.uk
Shout: www.giveusashout.org, text 85258
Young Minds: www.youngminds.org.uk

EUROPE
Mental Health Europe: www.mhe-sme.org
Mental Health Ireland: www.mentalhealthireland.ie

USA
HelpGuide: www.helpguide.org
Mentalhealth.gov: www.mentalhealth.gov
Mental Health America: www.mhanational.org
National Alliance on Mental Illness (NAMI): www.nami.org
National Institute of Mental Health: www.nimh.nih.gov
Very Well Mind: www.verywellmind.com

CANADA
Canadian Mental Health Association: cmha.ca
Crisis Service Canada: www.ementalhealth.ca

AUSTRALIA AND NEW ZEALAND
Beyond Blue: www.beyondblue.org.au
Head to Health: headtohealth.gov.au
Health Direct: www.healthdirect.gov.au
Mental Health Australia: mhaustralia.org
Mental Health Foundation of New Zealand: www.mentalhealth.org.nz
SANE Australia: www.sane.org

ANXIETY-SPECIFIC RESOURCES

In the following websites you can find guidance, support, advice and treatment options.

UK
Anxiety UK: www.anxietyuk.org.uk
No More Panic: www.nomorepanic.co.uk
No panic: www.nopanic.org.uk
Social Anxiety: www.social-anxiety.org.uk

USA
Anxiety and Depression Association of America: www.adaa.org

CANADA
Anxiety Canada: www.anxietycanada.com

AUSTRALIA AND NEW ZEALAND
Anxiety New Zealand Trust: www.anxiety.org.nz
Black Dog Institute: www.blackdoginstitute.org.au

SUPPORT FOR SUICIDAL THOUGHTS

If you are finding it difficult to cope or know someone who is, and need to be heard without judgment or pressure, you can find information and support from the following:

Crisis Text Line (US, Canada, Ireland, UK): www.crisistextline.org

UK
Campaign Against Living Miserably (CALM): www.thecalmzone.net
PAPYRUS (dedicated to the prevention of young suicide): www.papyrus-uk.org
The Samaritans: www.samaritans.org

USA
American Foundation for Suicide Prevention: afsp.org
National Suicide Prevention Lifeline: suicidepreventionlifeline.org

CANADA
Canada Suicide Prevention Crisis Service: www.crisisservicescanada.ca

AUSTRALIA AND NEW ZEALAND
Lifeline Australia: www.lifeline.org.au

PODCASTS

A selection of podcasts about depression, mental health, wellbeing and therapy:

- *Mad World*, Bryony Gordon
- *Feel Better, Live More*, Dr Chatterjee
- *Happy Place*, Fearne Cotton
- *Let's Talk about CBT*, Dr Lucy Maddox
- *Mental Health Foundation Podcasts*
- *People Soup*, Ross McIntosh
- *Psychologists off the Clock*, Debbie Sorensen, Diana Hill, Yael Schonbrun

BOOKS

BOOKS ABOUT PERSONAL EXPERIENCES OF DEPRESSION
Gordon, Bryony, *Mad Girl* (Headline, 2016)
Gordon, Bryony, *No Such Thing as Normal* (Headline, 2021)
Haig, Matt, *Reasons to Stay Alive* (Canongate, 2015)

BOOKS ABOUT WELLBEING, SELF-CARE OR TO INSPIRE
Bach, Richard, *Jonathan Livingston Seagull* (MacMillan, 1970)
Cain, Susan, *Quiet, The Power of Introverts in a World That Can't Stop Talking* (Viking, 2012)
Cotton, Fearne, *Quiet, Silencing the brain chatter and believing that you're good enough* (Orion Spring, 2018)
Mackesy, Charlie, *The Boy the Fox and the Mole* (Ebury, 2019)
Morgan, Adam and Barden, Mark, *A Beautiful Constraint* (Wiley, 2015)
Neill, Michael, *The Inside Out Revolution*, (Hay House, 2013)
Wax, Ruby, *How to be Human* (Penguin Life, 2018)

ABOUT US

Welbeck Balance publishes books dedicated to changing lives.
Our mission is to deliver life-enhancing books to help improve
your wellbeing so that you can live your life with greater clarity
and meaning, wherever you are on life's journey. Our Trigger
books are specifically devoted to opening up conversations
about mental health and wellbeing.

Welbeck Balance and Trigger are part of the Welbeck
Publishing Group – a globally recognized independent publisher
based in London. Welbeck are renowned for our innovative ideas,
production values and developing long-lasting content.
Our books have been translated into over 30 languages in
more than 60 countries around the world.

If you love books, then join the club and sign up
to our newsletter for exclusive offers, extracts,
author interviews and more information.

www.welbeckpublishing.com   **www.triggerhub.org**

- welbeckpublish   - Triggercalm
- welbeckpublish   - Triggercalm
- welbeckuk   - Triggercalm